CONNECTING
Holidays & Literature

Written by Deborah Plona Cerbus and Cheryl Feichtenbiner Rice

Illustrated by Cheryl Buhler, Paula Spence, Keith Vasconcelles, and Theresa Wright

Teacher Created Materials
P.O. Box 1214
Huntington Beach, CA 92647
©1992 Teacher Created Materials, Inc.
Made in U.S.A.

ISBN-1-55734-348-9

Table of Contents

Table of Contents *(cont.)*

Introduction

Connecting Holidays and Literature is a 144 page resource book which provides specific strategies and activities for integrating holiday activities with more than 30 related children's literature selections. It addresses two current trends in education: the whole language movement, and emphasis on integrating curriculum areas. Whole language philosophy stresses the use of literature to build literacy by connecting content areas. Many holidays are covered, including traditional holidays, such as Christmas and Thanksgiving, ethnic holidays, such as Kwanzaa and Cinco de Mayo, and special fun celebrations, such as Teddy Bear Day and Sandwich Day. By studying holidays, children will gain global awareness and an appreciation for cultural diversity.

Connecting Holidays and Literature includes the following sections:

> **Festive Fall**
>
> **Wonderful Winter**
>
> **Sparkling Spring**
>
> **Sizzling Summer**

Each section contains descriptions of picture books, a description of the holiday, related poetry and music. Directions for a variety of follow-up activities are included with supporting projects and pattern pages. An extensive bibliography for each section lists other titles appropriate for the season.

Follow-up activities extend and reinforce both the literature and the holiday concepts by using various forms of expression including:

poetry	**science activities**
graphing	**cooking**
art projects	**games**
writing	**dramatics**
murals	**brainstorming**

Some activities are individualized while others involve children in small cooperative learning groups. In addition to the four main sections, the appendices provide:

> **A format for a Holiday Handbook**
>
> **Poetry Pocket**
>
> **Classy Cookery**
>
> **Bibliography of resource books for teachers**

The goal of *Connecting Holidays and Literature* is to improve instruction in the primary classroom by utilizing holiday literature across the curriculum, providing hands-on activities that can easily be implemented, and sparking young children's interest in making each day a celebration.

School Days

Author: B. G. Hennessey

Publisher: Viking, 1990

Summary: The rhyming text and adorable illustrations work together to tell the story of an exciting, yet typical day at school in an early elementary classroom. Children and teachers will quickly recognize themselves and their busy schedules.

Related Holiday: The first day of school is traditionally an exciting celebration for young children, their families, and their teachers.

Related Poetry: ''Summer Goes'' by Russell Hoban, *The Family Read-Aloud Treasury* (Little, Brown & Company, 1991); ''Miss Norma Jean Pugh, First Grade Teacher'' by Mary O'Neill and ''The Creature in the Classroom'' by Jack Prelutsky, *The Random House Book of Poetry for Children* (Random House, 1983); traditional ''ABC Song'' and ''Counting'' by Lee Bennett Hopkins, *Side By Side: Poems to Read Together* (Simon & Schuster, 1988)

Related Songs: ''At My School'' by Barb Robinson and ''Transition Song'' by Diana Nazaruk, *Piggyback Songs* (Warren Publishing House, 1983); ''Kindergarten Here We Come'' and ''Off to Kindergarten'' by Valerie Bilesker, *More Piggyback Songs* (Warren Publishing House, 1984)

Connecting Activities:

- After you have read this book to your class, have them brainstorm a list of all the things and events that they have noticed in the book. Make a large schoolhouse shape from red tag board and add details with contrasting pieces of construction paper. Laminate the shape. Place the list on the schoolhouse. Use a water soluble overhead projector marker so that you may wash off the shape and use it year after year. A schoolhouse shape also makes a great shape book in which to write about the things children like to do in their class.

- If your children did not notice the rabbit which appears throughout the book during your initial reading, call their attention to it. The rabbit is mentioned only once in the text, but it adds an element of fun to the entire book. Have the children predict how many times the rabbit appears in the book. Then do an actual count. Challenge your students to find it as it races across each double-page spread of the story. Emphasize the importance of details in illustrations to make the story more exciting.

- Children may make a comparison chart to compare and contrast the classroom in the book with their own classroom. How are they alike? How are they different? Encourage children to think of items mentioned in the text, as well as items seen in the illustrations. Make a list of the items to be compared in the left column of your chart. Be sure to include items such as class pet, listing of daily plan, birthday board, helpers, show and tell, recess rules, etc. Make a heading for each of your three columns: Event, Classroom in the Book, Our Classroom. Show your comparison by using a yes or no in the appropriate column.

School Days (cont.)

• Create your own class story with a title such as "School Days in Room 3." Work with your class to write a text (either rhyming or narrative) that tells about a typical day in your classroom. Print each sentence at the bottom of a 12" x 18" (30 cm x 45 cm) sheet of white construction paper. Then have your students work to illustrate each page of text using crayons, markers, or ink outlines filled in with watercolors (as the illustrator did in the book). Children may work on the pages independently or with a partner, depending on the length of your text and the size of your class. Encourage students to add a lot of detail to their illustrations. Display stories around the classroom or assemble them into a class book.

• Assemble a photo display called "Our First Day of School" or "Our First Day in the First Grade." Take photographs of your students on the first day doing a variety of activities, such as those listed in the book. Mount each of the photographs on apple or school bus shapes (TCM732 — apple shape note pads and TCM730 — school bus shape note pads would make this quite simple) and display them on a bulletin board with appropriate captions. A border of apples or buses would add to the display. This would be an especially attractive addition to a beginning of the year parent night, or open house. Save these photos for use later in the year.

• Take photographs, similar to those mentioned above, at the end of the school year. Use the photographs from the beginning of the year and the end of the year to make a special end of the year folder for parents. Duplicate page 8 onto index paper to make a "Caring and Sharing Photo Folder" for each child to take home as a remembrance of the school year. Place the beginning of the year photo on the left hand side of the centerfold and place the end of the year photo on the right hand side of the centerfold. Children may decorate the outside of the folder and address it to their parents.

• As a beginning of the year getting acquainted activity, give each student a copy of page 9 in a manila envelope labeled with the student's name and directions, such as "Christina's Homework (Please help your child to complete this project and return it to school in this envelope on the next school day)." The children may then use their own invented spellings and artwork to tell about themselves, or they could dictate their thoughts to a parent and have their words written on the sheet. When the sheets come back to school, they could be mounted on pieces of construction paper and assembled into a class book, or they could be mounted into a pre-made hardcover book, such as those available from Treetop Publishing (see bibliography, page 144). Title your book and add it to your classroom library for all to enjoy.

School Days *(cont.)*

- Use heavy paper to prepare a schoolhouse shape cover for a class book called "Things We Like to Do in Grade _____." Give each student a page pre-cut in the same shape as the cover to make a schoolhouse-shaped book. At the bottom of the page, the children write their favorite thing about school in a sentence, such as, "At school I like to write stories."

- If you have older students, conduct an interest survey to find out the things that they would like to learn in your classroom. Vote on them to find the top five things which your students would like to learn about in your classroom. Keep the list and try to include in your plans as many of these ideas as possible during the year.

- Duplicate the certificate on page 10 and give a copy to each of your students on the first day of school to let them know how glad you are to have them in your class. You might duplicate the certificate on colored index paper or color in parts of it to make it more attractive.

- On the first day of school, send home a copy of a back-to-school poem, like the one to the right, along with a note telling the parents what things their children did on the first day of school. Have the parents encourage their children to talk about their day.

School Time

Now is the time
When summer ends,
We go to school
And make new friends.

—Cheryl Rice

- Before the school year begins, write a letter to each of your students telling them a little about your plans for the school year. Mail these to the children a few days before they are to report to school to begin establishing positive rapport with each student and to alleviate some of the back-to-school jitters. (Add a brief note to parents in the same envelope telling them that you are looking forward to working with them and perhaps letting them know the date of parent night.)

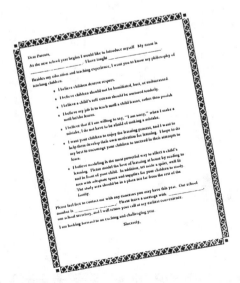

Caring and Sharing Photo Folder

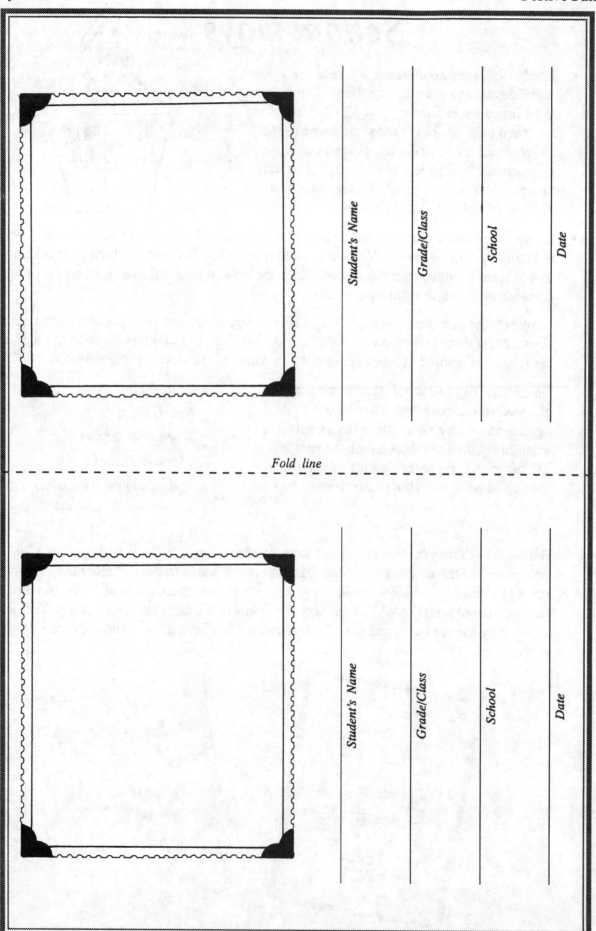

Student's Name

Grade/Class

School

Date

Fold line

Student's Name

Grade/Class

School

Date

Let's Learn About _____

(Child's Name)

Favorite school activity _____

Favorite sport _____

Favorite color _____

Favorite book _____

Favorite song _____

Sisters _____

Brothers _____

Pets _____

Favorite television show _____

Favorite game _____

Favorite restaurant _____

Favorite home activity _____

Back-to-School Certificate

This is to certify that _____ had a
　　　　　　　　　　　　　　name

TERRIFIC
First Day of School

and is an important member of our class.

_____
Teacher's Signature

_____
Grade/Class

_____
Date

Nana Upstairs & Nana Downstairs

Author: Tomie dePaola

Publisher: Penguin, 1973

Summary: This is a beautiful story about the relationship between a young boy, his grandmother, and his great-grandmother.

Now One Foot, Now the Other

Author: Tomie dePaola

Publisher: G. P. Putnam's Sons

Summary: A young boy named Bobby helps his grandfather learn how to walk again after he has a stroke.

Related Holiday: Grandparents' Day is a national holiday in the United States, held in September on the first Sunday after Labor Day. It is a special day to express our love for Grandma and Grandpa.

Related Poetry: ''Grandpa Dropped His Glasses'' by Leroy F. Jackson and ''Growing Old'' by Rose Henderson, *The Random House Book of Poetry for Children* (Random House, 1983).

Related Songs: ''Grandma's Coming Soon to Visit'' by Jean Warren, *Special Day Celebrations*, (Warren Publishing House, 1989)

Connecting Activities:

- Compare and contrast the two books. Talk about the ways in which the grandparents are similar, and how they are different. Discuss the changes that take place as people age. Stress the fact that although grandparents may sometimes act or talk differently because of advanced age or illness, they are still the same people we have always loved. This is a good opportunity for students to talk about feelings they may have, especially if they have a grandparent who is ill, or if they've experienced the death of a grandparent. You might have the school counselor or someone from a local council on aging visit to discuss any fears or concerns that students may express.

- Some of the students may have grandparents who are retired. Discuss what retirement means and talk about the benefits of having extra leisure time. Make a list of fun activities for grandparents to do during retirement (fishing, golf, crafts, reading, etc.). It might be fun to send a copy of the list home to be given to grandparents. Make a class book called ''Our 3-R's of Retirement.'' Have each student write a sentence and draw illustrations for a page, telling one of his or her favorite ideas for retirement fun.

Nana Upstairs & Nana Downstairs; Now One Foot, Now the Other *(cont.)*

- Both books stressed the idea of grandparents and grandchildren learning from each other and helping each other. List ways that grandparents help us and brainstorm a list of ways that we can help our grandparents. In many communities it is possible for a class to "adopt" residents from a nursing home. The class would visit their older friends periodically and send cards and decorations for holidays. During the visits, a class may play games with their older friends, read to them, sing songs, or even perform a play. Friendships that develop between the students and their senior friends are very beneficial to everyone, and help the students to have respect and a good attitude toward senior citizens.

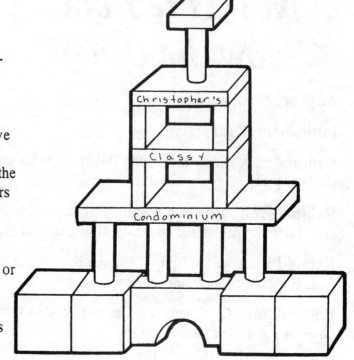

- The grandson and grandfather in *Now One Foot, Now the Other* build block towers together. Organize a block building cooperative group activity in your classroom. Provide a variety of sizes and shapes of wooden blocks and other materials, such as plastic connecting blocks. If you do not have a supply of building blocks, ask a kindergarten teacher if you may borrow some for the day. Measure the heights of the block towers and graph them from the lowest to the highest. The heights can be represented by strings or strips of adding machine tape and can be arranged in order on a bulletin board or wall. Make signs for the buildings, giving them unique names, such as "Christopher's Classy Condominium." Invite other classes to see your block city.

- Set up an author's center featuring Tomie dePaola. Include a collection of his many books and discuss with students how the stories relate to his real life, his family, and his Italian heritage.

- Have students write thank you notes to grandparents on the stationery provided on page 14. Included in the note could be some comments thanking grandparents for something they have done or taught their grandchildren.

- Grandparents are special people for many reasons. It's a nice idea to invite them into the classroom to share in some of their grandchildren's activities. The ideas on the following page will get you started in planning your own celebration for Grandparents' Day. (Note: For any of these activities, it's important for all children to have a guest. Always send a note home to parents describing the celebration and asking for children without grandparents to bring another friend or relative. You'll find that grandparents who visit school are often willing to adopt another grandchild for the day.)

Nana Upstairs & Nana Downstairs;
Now One Foot, Now the Other (cont.)

- Ask students to bring a grandparent to visit the class. Have the grandparent share a song, a game, or a story that was popular when he or she was a child. It's always fascinating for young children to hear how different things were years ago. They might be interested in hearing how schools were different, and what grandparents did for fun after school. Interview the grandparents using questions prepared by the students ahead of time. Ask the grandparents to show a photograph of themselves from when they were in school. Invite grandparents to sign up as volunteers in your classroom to help listen to students read or to help with baking or craft projects.

- Hold a Grandparents' Gala and perform a short program or play for your guests. Have students recite poetry and sing the song listed on page 11. Other ideas for activities include having a sing-along, reading stories together, or working with math materials such as pattern blocks.

- Try a "Family Heritage Day" to talk about ancestry and family trees. (Note: If you have adopted children in your classroom, talk with the parents ahead of time to see how they would like the activity handled.) Send a note home asking for information on what countries the students' ancestors came from. On a large world map, locate the countries and label them with the family name. Invite a family member to come as a guest speaker, sharing information about his or her heritage.

- Make grandparents feel welcome by hanging a large banner for the celebration. Students may color and decorate the banner with crayons or markers. As grandparents leave, give them a small token of appreciation for attending Grandparents' Day, such as a card or a flower.

Stationery

Dear Grandparent,

_____

_____

_____

_____

_____

_____

_____

_____

Love,

_____

Follow the Dream

Author: Peter Sis

Publisher: Alfred A. Knopf, 1991

Summary: Travel with Columbus to the new world, and learn about the history behind the historic voyage. The beautiful and intricate illustrations reflect the artistic style prevalent in Columbus' day.

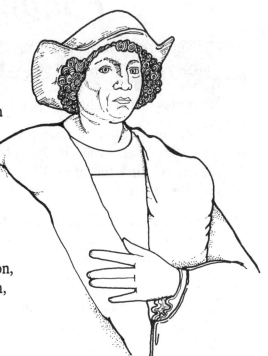

Related Holiday: Columbus Day is celebrated on October 12th in both North America and South America in honor of his voyage in 1492.

Related Poetry: ''Columbus Day'' by Myra Cohn Livingston, *Celebrations* (Scholastic, 1985); ''Land Ahoy'' by Jean Warren, *Special Day Celebrations* (Warren Publishing House, 1989)

Connecting Activities:

- Use a K-W-L chart to determine how much information the students know about Christopher Columbus. You need three sheets of chart paper to record the following: what the students **know** (K), what they **want to know** (W), and after reading the book, what they **learned** (L). At the end of the unit, go back to the chart and star information which was correct. Consult other factual books and encyclopedias to answer questions that did not get answered by reading *Follow the Dream*.

- Discuss the author's interesting introductory letter which talks about his reasons for writing the book. The book jacket provides good biographical information and mentions the research involved in writing the book.

- Another excellent book about Columbus is *The First Voyage of Christopher Columbus, 1492* by Barry Smith (see bibliography, page 43). Each page features a small map showing the location of Columbus' ships during the voyage in different colors. Make copies of the world map on pages 64 and 65. Use a small cut-out ship to trace the route that he took.

- Laminate a world map and trace Columbus' route with a wipe-off marker. Find out about Columbus' other voyages to the new world. Trace each voyage in a different color.

- Figure out how many days it took Columbus to complete his voyage. Move a small ship on the world map every few days to indicate how far the ship would have gone. To conceptualize the differences between a round or flat world, take the small world maps mentioned above and staple them into a cylindrical shape. Talk about the differences between a flat map which is rectangular and a globe which is spherical. Find examples of rectangles, spheres, and cylinders in your classroom and school.

- Locate Italy and Spain on a map. Discuss how these countries are part of the continent of Europe. Ask students if they can name the continent on which they live. Name and locate the other continents.

Follow the Dream (cont.)

- Columbus enlisted the aid of the King and Queen of Spain for his journey. Do some royal research with this activity. Make a large crown shape out of yellow tagboard. Use a hot glue gun to attach decorations such as sequins or inexpensive costume jewels. On the crown, list countries that have had kings, queens, or other rulers. Star the countries which still have royalty.

- Using tag board, trace and enlarge the ship on page 17. On the ship, list and illustrate about five or six important events in Columbus' life. Display the ship on a bulletin board or in a Columbus center as a time line of his life. Add waves made of blue tag board to the bottom of the ship for a realistic effect.

- Color and add details to the Ship Shape on page 17 to represent one of Columbus' ships. Give the ship a new name. On the bottom portion of the ship, draw all of the things that you would take on a long sea voyage. Be sure to include essential items such as food, water, and medicines.

- Columbus followed his dream by sailing across the ocean and discovering an unknown land. Ask students to pretend that they are explorers with a dream. Students can complete this sentence, ''I would like to follow my dream by...'' Illustrate sentences and compile them into a class book or display them on a bulletin board. Add the caption ''Following Our Dreams'' on cloud shapes.

- In the 1400's, weaving was an important trade. Columbus' father was a weaver. Weave some simple placements to demonstrate this craft. First fold a 12" x 18" (30 cm x 45 cm) sheet of construction paper in half. Then cut wavy or straight lines about 1" (2.5 cm) apart from the fold to 1" (2.5 cm) away from the top edge of the paper. Unfold the sheet to make the weaving mat. Emphasize the over and under pattern of weaving. Try weaving other types of material through the mat such as brightly colored yarn, rick-rack, or lace. Invite someone who is a weaver to come in and demonstrate this craft.

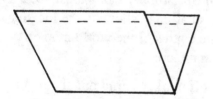 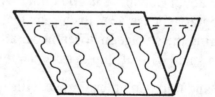 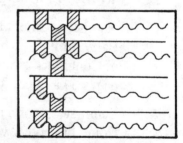

- Create a Columbus collage showing many facts about Columbus' life. Start out by doing a word web with the word Columbus in the center. Think of as many words as you can that relate to his life. Then write the word Columbus in the center of a 12" x 18" (30 cm x 45 cm) piece of construction paper. Encourage the children to use fancy lettering in the style of calligraphy. Add pictures made from scrap materials and construction paper which represent events from his life. (For example, a boat, a piece of cloth, a crown, and the shape of the country of Italy.)

- To honor the memory of this great explorer, create a special commemorative stamp or coin (page 18). Children may use crayons or markers to depict Columbus' contribution to history.

Ship Shape

Directions: Enlarge and use this ship to create a bulletin board, book cover, or for the activities on page 16.

Commemorate Columbus!

Directions: Using crayons or markers, decorate the coin and stamp to show Columbus' contribution to history.

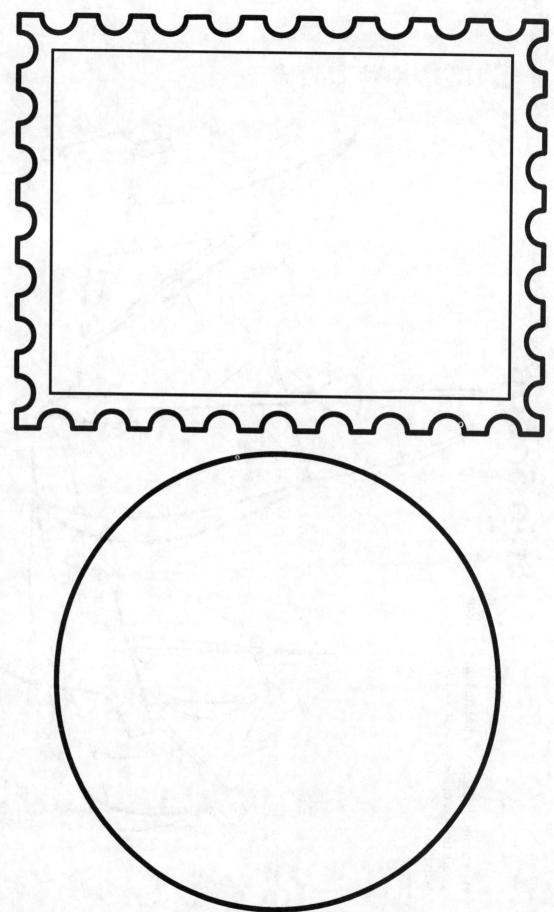

The Biggest Pumpkin Ever

Author: Steven Kroll

Publisher: Scholastic, 1984

Summary: Two mice work together to grow the biggest pumpkin ever seen at the town pumpkin contest. The story stresses the ideas of friendship and cooperation.

Related Holiday: Halloween is celebrated on October 31st and is sometimes called All Hallow's Eve.

Related Poetry: ''October Fun'' and ''Pumpkin Head'' by Aileen Fisher, *Out in the Dark and Daylight* (Harper and Row, 1980)

Related Songs: ''I'm a Little Pumpkin'' by Barbara Hasson and ''I Picked a Pumpkin'' by Sue Brown, *Holiday Piggyback Songs* (Warren Publishing House, 1988)

Connecting Activities:

- Before reading the story, read the title and ask students what they think the book will be about. Or, have a real pumpkin hidden in a box and give some clues, asking students to guess what's in the mystery box. Read the story after revealing the pumpkin. Brainstorm a list of words that relate to pumpkins. Write them on small pieces of paper and tape them to the pumpkin.

- While reading the story, try to predict what will happen to the pumpkin as the two mice care for it. Have the class vote on whether they think the pumpkin should be used for the contest, as Clayton wants, or as a jack-o-lantern, as Desmond had planned to do. This information could be displayed as a two column picture graph, done with plain paper pumpkins and jack-o-lantern faces.

- Set up a pumpkin learning center in your classroom. First, stuff a large orange trash bag with newspaper and add a face with construction paper to create a giant jack-o-lantern. (At Halloween time, some stores carry trash bags which already have a jack-o-lantern face printed on them.) Include in your center picture books about pumpkins as well as some informational texts.

- Take your class on a field trip to a pumpkin patch. Look at the vine and how the pumpkins are attached to it. See if you can find some pumpkins which are still green. Choose a pumpkin to take back to your class to decorate or carve for Halloween. Use the pumpkin for math activities. Students can estimate the weight and the circumference of the pumpkin and the number of seeds it contains. Check your predictions by weighing and measuring the pumpkin and grouping the seeds by tens for counting. Or, put some seeds or pumpkin shaped candies in a jar for estimating.

The Biggest Pumpkin Ever *(cont.)*

- Talk about the life cycle of a pumpkin (seed, sprout, plant, flower, pumpkin). Work in small groups of three or four students and have each group illustrate with crayon or marker a part of the cycle on a sheet of white index paper. Write a sentence at the bottom of each page to describe the stage of growth. To display the finished products, staple the pictures onto large pumpkin shapes and add the caption "How a Pumpkin Grows."

- Have a pumpkin decorating contest in your classroom or school. Students may add details with markers, paint, and even props to create people, animals, etc. The only rule is that the pumpkin may not be carved. Display the pumpkins in your lobby or entryway, and form a panel of judges, one from each grade level. Give each pumpkin an award for being the most creative, the neatest, the funniest, etc.

- Read *Mousekin's Golden House* by Edna Miller (see bibliography, page 43) and compare it to *The Biggest Pumpkin Ever*. Compare and contrast the behavior of the mice in each book. In which book are the characters more real? Why? List some of the behaviors of Desmond and Clayton which make the story a fantasy (mice wearing clothes, driving cars, etc.).

- Save some of the pumpkin seeds for a variety of activities. Try roasting some of the seeds for a special snack. Wash and dry the seeds thoroughly and mix them with two or three tablespoons of cooking oil (just enough to coat the seeds lightly). Spread the seeds out on a cookie sheet. Sprinkle with salt and roast in an oven at 350° F (180° C) until lightly browned (about 10-20 minutes depending on the amount of seeds). Stir the seeds occasionally while baking. Cooked this way, the seeds have a crunchy popcorn-like taste. Record the recipe in the Classy Cookery recipe book (see appendix, page 141).

- Try planting some pumpkin seeds in your science center. In addition to having each student grow a plant, try this experiment. Bring in four established plants. Put the first in a dark place, giving it plain water. Place the second in a light place, feeding it sugar water. The third should be set in a light place, but given plain water. Place the fourth in a light place, but give it fertilizer as well as water. Have the students predict which plant will show the best growth. Check the plants periodically and record the changes in a science journal (see appendix, page 143).

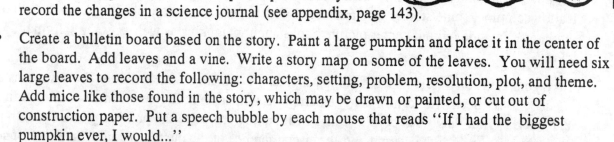

- Create a bulletin board based on the story. Paint a large pumpkin and place it in the center of the board. Add leaves and a vine. Write a story map on some of the leaves. You will need six large leaves to record the following: characters, setting, problem, resolution, plot, and theme. Add mice like those found in the story, which may be drawn or painted, or cut out of construction paper. Put a speech bubble by each mouse that reads "If I had the biggest pumpkin ever, I would..."

- Use the pumpkin patch activity sheet (page 21) to record a story map. Students record the important events from the story on the pumpkin shapes. Students can take the paper home and retell the story to their families.

Pumpkin Patch Story

See page 20 for directions.

Funnybones

Author: Janet and Allan Ahlberg

Publisher: Mulberry Books, 1980

Summary: This book tells of the adventure had by three skeletons (an adult, a child, and a dog) who go for a walk on a dark, dark night.

Related Holiday: Halloween is celebrated on October 31st in Great Britain, Ireland, Canada, and the United States as the evening before the feast of All Saint's Day.

Related Poetry: "Skeleton Parade" by Jack Prelutsky and "On Halloween" by Aileen Fisher, *Read-Aloud Rhymes for the Very Young* (Alfred A. Knopf, 1986); "Halloween" by Ivy O. Eastwick and "Look at That!" by Lilian Moore, *Side by Side: Poems to Read Together* (Simon & Schuster, 1988)

Related Songs: Traditional song "Dem Bones"

Connecting Activities:

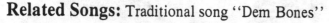

- As you read this book to your class, call attention to the skeletons of different animals. Encourage your students to guess what these animals are.

- Discuss with your students why the authors named the book *Funnybones*. Have your students vote as to whether they like this title or whether they would have given it another title. What other titles do your students believe would be suitable for the story?

- Discuss the idiom "tickled my funnybone" with your class and exactly where one's funnybone is. Decide if there really is a bone called the funnybone in the human skeleton. Verify your decision by checking in a reference book.

- Read several other books to your class that follow the same dark, dark pattern, such as *A Dark Dark Tale* by Ruth Brown and *In a Dark, Dark Wood* by June Melser and Joy Cowley (see bibliography, page 43). Compare and contrast the story elements such as location, setting, atmosphere created by the artwork, and ending.

- Make writing innovations following the same "dark, dark" pattern. Children may write their own individual innovations, or you could guide the children in writing a class innovation by writing the sentences suggested by your students on sentence strips and placing them in a pocket chart for all to read.

- Have your students create their own skeletons using white straws or foam packing peanuts. Children may make individual human skeletons on 12" x 18" (30 cm x 45 cm) pieces of black construction paper. These skeletons may be displayed on a long bulletin board or in the hallway along a tackstrip. (You might copy the poem "Skeleton Parade" by Jack Prelutsky on a large sheet of chart paper to display with your students' skeletons to create your own parade of skeletons.)

Funnybones (cont.)

- For a fun variation, encourage your students to make a mural of zoo animal skeletons, similar to the ones found in the book, by using white chalk on a long piece of black butcher paper. Have children guess what animals their classmates created. Make labels to identify the animals, but hide the words under the flap to check their guess.

- Do a K-W-L activity with your students. List, on a chart, the facts that they **know** about skeletons. Have them decide what they **want to know** about them. Invite a doctor or nurse to come into the classroom to explain the importance of the skeleton, as well as how the bones, joints and muscles work together. Read factual books such as *A Book About Your Skeleton* by Ruth Belov Gross, *The Skeleton Inside You* by Phillip Balestrino, *What's Inside My Body?* by DK Direct Limited, and *The Magic School Bus Inside the Human Body* by Joanna Cole (see bibliography, page 43). Have your students list on the chart what they have **learned** about skeletons.

- Ask students to estimate how many bones there are in the human skeleton. Bring a model skeleton into your classroom and count the exact number of bones (206). Verify your count by checking in a reference book. Compare your estimation to the actual number.

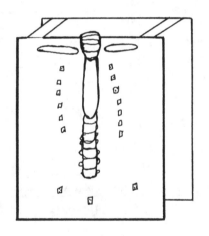

- Attach labels to the major bones on a life-size skeleton or on a cardboard skeleton posted in the room. You could make a ''sandwich-board'' learning center activity for the science area in your classroom. Use two sheets of 18" x 24" (46 cm x 61 cm) white tag board (one for the front and one for the back). Use two strips of 3" x 8" (8 cm x 20 cm) white tag board to attach the front and the back pieces together at the shoulders. Draw the outline of the body on the front and back with a marker. Cut bones out of the other scraps of tag board. Laminate the ''sandwich-board,'' the connecting strips, and the bones. Attach the bones to the correct places on the front and back of the body pieces with Velcro®. Children remove and then replace the bones to the ''sandwich-board'' while one child wears it.

- Assess your students' understanding of the human skeleton by having them complete the Human Skeleton activity on page 24.

- TCM570 — *Big Book of Science Charts: My Body* contains a pull-out chart of the human skeleton. Included are several related activities to do with children to extend learning.

The Human Skeleton

Directions: Label the skeleton parts by writing the words from the box on the lines.

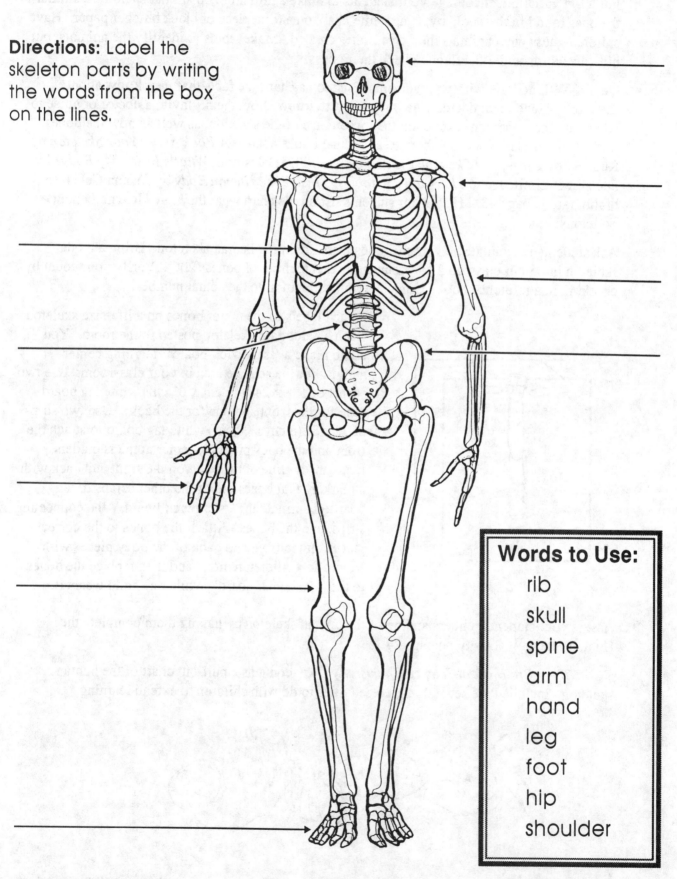

Words to Use:
rib
skull
spine
arm
hand
leg
foot
hip
shoulder

The Giant Jam Sandwich

Author: John Vernon Lord

Publisher: Houghton Mifflin, 1972

Summary: The residents of Itching Down solve their problem with four million wasps in a most unusual and creative way.

Related Holiday: Sandwich Day originated in England on October 14, 1744, to honor the Earl of Sandwich; Bread Day is celebrated on November 17th.

Related Poetry: "Peanut Butter Batter Bread" by Arnold Adoff, *Eats Poems* (Lothrop, Lee, and Shepard, 1979)

Related Songs: "Making Bread" and "I'm Going to Make a Sandwich" by Elizabeth McKinnon, *Special Day Celebrations* (Warren Publishing House, 1989); "Sandwiches" by Bob King, *The Book of Kid's Songs 2* (Klutz Press, 1989)

Connecting Activities:

- Introduce the story by discussing the history of the sandwich. It is thought to be invented by the Earl of Sandwich who is given credit for the idea of putting meat between two slices of bread.

- Draw the shape of a large slice of bread on brown tag board. Cut out and laminate the bread pattern so that it can be written on with a wipe-off pen. Have the class brainstorm a list of possible ingredients that you could put on a sandwich. Or, try to make a list of words which describe bread. Introduce the story *Sam's Sandwich* by David Pelham (see bibliography, page 43) which tells about a sandwich with some unexpected ingredients.

- After reading *The Giant Jam Sandwich*, do a story grammar on bread shapes. You will need six slices of bread to list the following: characters, setting, problem, resolution, theme, and plot (a few main events from the story). Have the students illustrate the parts of the story grammar.

- Many restaurants create sandwiches and name them after famous people. Have the students invent some new specialties named after celebrities with whom they are familiar. For example, a sandwich called the Mickey Mouse Melt might feature several varieties of cheese. Have each student write out a detailed recipe, beginning with a list of ingredients. Following the ingredient list, write the sequence of steps needed to make the sandwich. Compile the recipes into a class recipe book called "Celebrity Sandwiches." Have students illustrate the cookbook, make copies, and send home.

- Look in the *Guiness Book of Records* to find out some details about the world's largest loaf of bread (see bibliography, page 43). The book also contains fascinating facts about other foods, such as the largest pizza and the heaviest chocolate Easter egg.

The Giant Jam Sandwich *(cont.)*

- Have students work in small cooperative groups of four or five to find the most efficient and quickest way to make a peanut butter and jelly sandwich. Each group can pretend to form a sandwich company and can give their group a name, such as P. B. J., Ltd. After hearing each group's ideas of what worked and what the problems were, talk about how factories use an assembly line. Time how long it takes each group to make five sandwiches using its original approach. Then compare that time to the time it takes to make five sandwiches using an assembly line. Another variation is to try the same activity with partners and then groups of three. The completed sandwiches can be eaten for lunch or donated to another class as a healthy snack.

- Talk with the students about the sequence of events in the story. List the main events in order on a piece of chart paper. Then have each student color and cut out the pieces for the sandwich sequence game (page 28). The "sandwich" pieces are put in order as the story is retold. The students can practice the game in partners and then take their sandwich pieces home in a plastic sandwich bag. One extra game can be kept for use in a reading or story center.

- Sandwiches provide a great opportunity for connecting with math activities involving geometric shapes and fractions. Working with proper squares to represent a sandwich, cut the squares in half three different ways (horizontally, vertically, diagonally). Talk about the resulting rectangle and triangle shapes, and the different ways to represent a half (one-half, ½). Start over with some new squares of paper to work on thirds and fourths. If you use a circle shape to represent a sandwich such as a hamburger, you can talk about smaller fractions such as one-eighth.

- Use the book *Bread Bread Bread* by Ann Morris (see bibliography, page 43) to celebrate Bread Day. After the story is read, use a world map or globe to locate all the countries mentioned. Bring in an assortment of the breads from the story for the students to taste. Do a bar graph or picture graph to show the favorite bread of your class.

The Giant Jam Sandwich *(cont.)*

- Bring in some cookbooks and compare and contrast the ingredients that are found in different kinds of bread. Find out which ingredients are common in most breads. Talk about yeast and how it works. The yeast digests the flour and produces carbon dioxide which causes the bread to rise. A similar effect can be obtained by putting baking soda and vinegar in a soft drink bottle and putting a balloon over the top. The carbon dioxide produced will expand the balloon.

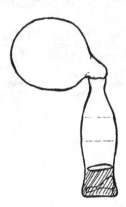

- In your science corner, try some experiments with growing mold on bread. This is easily done by moistening a piece of bread and putting it in a tightly closed container. Keep the container in a warm, dark place for about a week. Try some other jars in sunlight and in a cold refrigerator. Compare the results.

- Play a sandwich relay game. For each team you will need the following sandwich pieces cut out from felt or laminated tag board: two brown bread slices, a green lettuce leaf, a tomato slice, and a pink circle or square to represent lunch meat. The ingredients are laid out on the floor in a line. Putting each ingredient on a paper plate that has been securely taped to the floor works well. The object of the game is for each team member to pick up one ingredient at a time to assemble a sandwich. At the end of the line, the student pretends to take a bite, then takes the sandwich apart and returns the pieces to the plates on the way back to the team. The first team to "eat" all their sandwiches is the winner.

- Finish your celebration of this holiday by organizing a "Super Sandwich" lunch for the class. Talk about Dagwood, the comic strip character who makes huge sandwiches. Create some of your own for your lunch. As a special addition, bake your own bread for your sandwiches or visit a local bakery to see the process. Weigh and measure your sandwiches. Finally, enjoy eating them.

Sandwich Sequence Game

Directions: Write the main events of the story on the sandwich pieces. Put the pieces in order and retell the story.

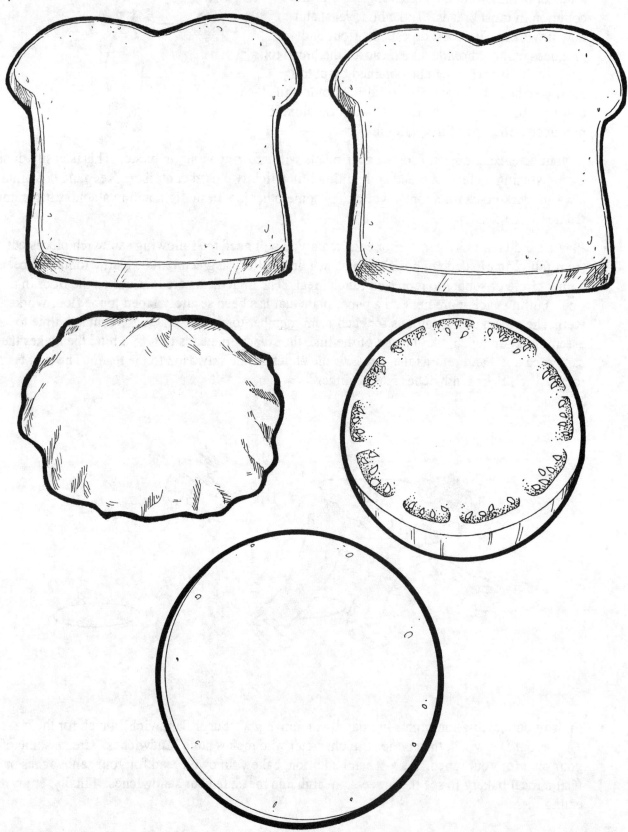

Just Open a Book

Author: P. K. Hallinan

Publisher: Childrens Press, 1981

Summary: The clever verse and humorous illustrations in this book tell of the varied adventures one can have by opening a book.

Related Holiday: National Children's Book Week is celebrated during the third week in November to celebrate the joy found in reading good books. This celebration began as ''Good Book Week'' in 1916. Books could also be celebrated during a ''March is Reading Month'' celebration.

Related Poetry: ''The Reason I Like Chocolate'' by Nikki Giovanni, ''Keep a Poem in Your Pocket'' by Beatrice Schenk De Regniers and ''Hello Book!'' by N. M. Bodecker, *The Family Read-Aloud Holiday Treasury* (Little, Brown & Company, 1991); ''A Merry Literary Christmas'' by Alice Low, *The Family Read-Aloud Christmas Treasury* (Little, Brown & Company, 1989)

Related Song: See original song ''B-O-O-K-S!'' by Cheryl Rice on page 30.

Connecting Activities:

- As you read the book to your students, be ready to explain who some of the characters are, since the prior knowledge of your students will be varied. Place books which tell about the characters in *Just Open a Book* in a ''Book Week Center'' for students to have adventures with them.

- Children may use the titles of their favorite books to create a ''Favorite Books Quilt.'' Display it in your classroom or hallway during Book Week. Give each child a 6" (15 cm) square piece of white construction paper on which the child can draw a picture that tells about his or her favorite book. Write a sentence, such as ''My favorite book is _____ by _____.'' Mount these 6" squares on a variety of 7" (18 cm) squares of colorful construction paper. Mount squares on a bulletin board as a quilt or try the following idea for a three-dimensional quilt. For the background of your quilt, use a bright yellow 36" x 48" (91 cm x 102 cm) piece of synthetic felt and stitch a simple piece of lacy, white cotton trim around all four edges. Attach the students' favorite book squares together with rolled paper tape that will allow you to reuse the quilt background again for other projects. Give your quilt a title such as ''Our Favorite Book Quilt'' and display it proudly.

- Bring a large gift-wrapped box into your classroom filled with some of your favorite books to give your students a special gift of reading. Read some of these to the class during this celebration. Tell your students why they are your favorite books. Encourage your students (if age-appropriate) to practice reading their favorite books. Share them with the class or a partner.

Just Open a Book (cont.)

- Visit the school or public library to learn about books, magazines, reference materials, the card catalog, and other unique features of the library. Have the librarian tell about his or her job.

- Make a class book and title it "Why Do We Like to Read?" Ask each child why he or she likes to read. You may write down the response, or the child may write it. Take a photograph of each child reading a favorite book to attach to each child's page in the book. Design a colorful book jacket for the class book.

- Help your students learn the song "B-O-O-K-S!" that is sung to the tune of "B-I-N-G-O!"

There was a class
That loved to read,
And books were what they read oh.
B-O-O-K-S, B-O-O-K-S, B-O-O-K-S
And books were what they read oh.

- Discuss and locate the different parts of a book, including the title, author, illustrator, publisher, copyright, and dedication. Have students assemble the mini-books on pages 32 and 33. Each student chooses a favorite book, finds the different parts of the book, and records the information on the appropriate mini-book page. To prepare mini-books, copy pages 32-33 back to back. Make one copy per student. Cut the page in half along the dashed line. Place the bottom half (pages 6, 3) beneath the top (pages 8, 1). Fold along the solid line and staple.

- Read several Caldecott and Newbery Award winners to your class. Discuss these awards and their significance. Ask your librarian for a list of these winners.

- Designate one day during National Children's Book Week as "Poetry Day." Read poetry to your class throughout the day. Be sure to include non-rhyming as well as rhyming poetry. Read the Beatrice Schenk de Regniers poem, "Keep a Poem in Your Pocket." Then make and send home a "Poetry Pocket" (see page 142) with some of the students' favorite poems inside, so that they can share poetry with their families.

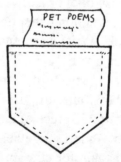

- Have your students create their own bookmarks to advertise National Children's Book Week. Duplicate these bookmarks on colored index paper and deliver them to other classes at your school.

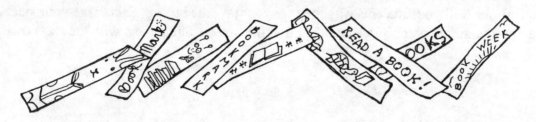

Just Open a Book (cont.)

- Trade classrooms with another teacher (preferably a different grade level) during story time one day. Together, select an appropriate book and try some of the following activities to culminate your Book Week celebration.

    — Have a reading party in your classroom. Sometime during the week prior to the party, give each student a "Ticket to Reading Success" as a reward for his or her reading progress that will be good for the purchase of a bag of popcorn at the party (explain the party to your students ahead of time). Set aside a period of time suitable to the age of your students (20 minutes - 1 hour) during which they may read materials of their choice from home or from school. Children may bring pillows to use and sit anywhere in the classroom, as long as they spend their time reading. For a special treat, pop some popcorn which the children may purchase with the tickets you have given them. You might serve a cold drink, too.

    — Plan a "Picture Book Day" with other classrooms (at about the same grade level). Each teacher of the participating classes chooses one of his or her favorite picture books on which to focus. Children from all of the participating classes are divided into groups so that they can rotate into all of the involved classrooms during this day. (If there are three classrooms participating, then each of the three teachers divides his or her class into three equal groups; 1, 2, 3. All of the 1's form a group, all of the 2's are a group, all of the 3's are a group. These three groups rotate into the three classrooms.) Determine the time spent in each classroom and a rotation schedule ahead of time. The teacher might dress as a character from the book. The teacher reads the book to each group of children and then does a variety of activities with them (all of which relate to their particular book): songs, poetry, art projects, flannelboard stories, storytelling, or learning games. What a fun conclusion to National Children's Book Week!

Mini-Book

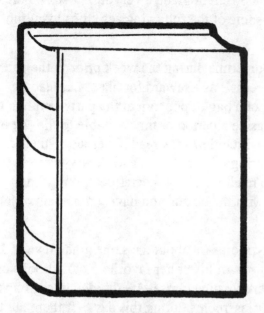

I found my favorite pages in the book.

8

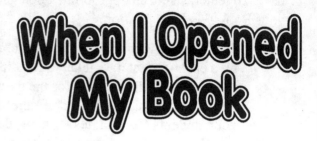

By _____

1

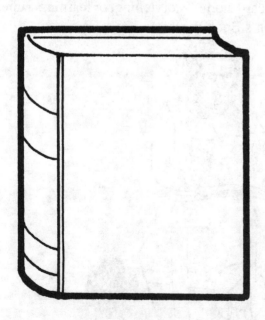

I found its copyright date.

6

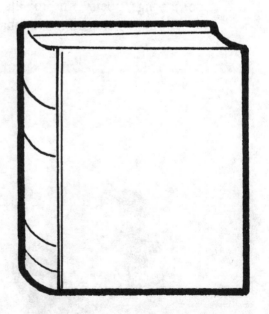

I found its author.

3

Mini-Book *(cont.)*

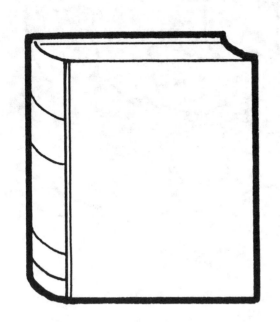

I found its title.

2

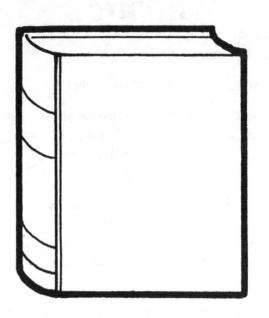

I found its dedication.

7

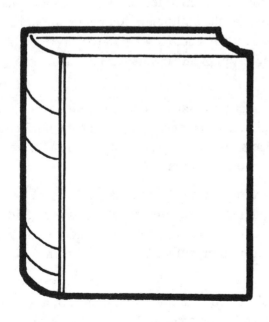

I found its illustrator.

4

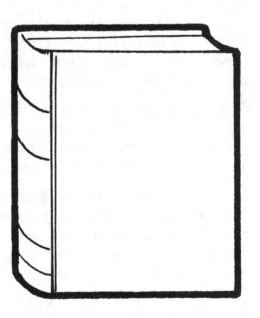

I found its publisher.

5

The Teddy Bears' Picnic

Author: Jimmy Kennedy

Publisher: Green Tiger Press, 1983

Summary: Join the teddy bears as they picnic in the woods on a lovely summer day. The surprise ending reveals some unexpected guests at the festivities.

Related Holiday: Teddy Bear Day is celebrated October 27th in honor of the birthday of former President Theodore Roosevelt, after whom teddy bears were named.

Related Poetry: ''Grandpa Bear's Lullaby'' by Jane Yolen and ''My Teddy Bear'' by Marchette Chute, *Bear in Mind, A Book of Bear Poems* (Puffin Books, 1989)

Related Songs: ''Teddy Bear, Teddy Bear'' adapted traditional, *Special Day Celebrations* (Warren Publishing House, Inc., 1989); ''That Bear Makes Me Crazy'' by Kevin Roth, *Unbearable Bears* (cassette tape, Marlboro Records, 1986)

Connecting Activities:

- Bring in a large picnic basket which contains the book, some small teddy bears and some picnic items such as a picnic cloth, napkins, and toy dishes. Let the children predict what might be in your basket. Make a list of the guesses and star the items that actually are in the basket. To create an outdoor mood while reading the story, spread out picnic cloths or blankets for the students to sit on as they listen to the story.

- Give each student a few teddy bear shaped cookies or candy to snack on during the story. Put some in a jar and use for estimating. Record the estimates on a paper teddy bear shape. These treats can also be used for counting and story problems. For example, five teddy bears were walking in the forest and two climbed up a tree. How many were left?

- Check prior knowledge by asking the students if they know the origin of the teddy bear. See if they know who Theodore (Teddy) Roosevelt is and tell them how the teddy bear was named after him. The story goes that he refused to shoot a bear cub on a hunting trip, and the cub was named ''Teddy's Bear.'' Soon afterwards, stores began to manufacture teddy bears in Roosevelt's honor.

- As you are reading the story, ask the children to look carefully and to estimate how many teddy bears appear throughout the book. Have the students take turns counting the bears on each page and total the amounts. After the story is read, cut six large paw prints out of construction paper to list the elements of a story grammar (characters, setting, problem, resolution, theme, and plot). Work as a whole class or in small groups to complete the story grammar.

The Teddy Bears' Picnic (cont.)

- Put up a large laminated bear shape on a bulletin board or chalkboard. Brainstorm a list of as many bears as you can, including both real bears and fictional bears that you might find in literature or on television. The students can draw or paint pictures of the bears on the list and put them around the large bear shape on a bulletin board. Add a caption such as ''Meet Our V.I.B.'s'' (very important bears) and add a border decorated with bears (available at teacher supply stores).

- Make a ''beary'' special display in your classroom by putting out a collection of bears and books on a picnic cloth. Be sure to include narrative stories as well as non-fiction books about real bears. Invite someone who collects or makes bears to visit the classroom to talk about bear collecting, which has become a very popular hobby.

- On Teddy Bear Day, have the students bring their bears to school. When the bears arrive, let the students weigh and measure their bears. Represent the heights with strings or strips of paper and arrange them in order from shortest to tallest. The information can be recorded on a paper teddy bear shape and taken home. Give each bear a prize for being the smallest, funniest, happiest; whatever title is appropriate. Have a picnic with the bears. Enjoy snacks such as honey and biscuits. Take pictures of the bears at the picnic and make a photo essay class book. Add humorous captions under each photograph. Don't forget to take a group photo for the end of the book.

- Work in size-appropriate cooperative groups to research different types of bears (Alaskan brown bears, grizzly bears, polar bears, etc.). Provide the students with encyclopedias and other non-fiction texts to gather as much information as they can about their bears. Students can name their research group to represent the bear being studied (for example, the ''Growling Grizzlies.'') The reports should include information on the bear's habitat, size, foods, color, and unique habits. Groups may include a project such as a mural, a poster, or a short skit. Present reports to another class.

- In the story, the ending reveals some people dressed in bear costumes and masks who attended the picnic. Reproduce the bear mask on page 37 onto large index paper. Color and cut it out. Glue a craft stick to the bottom. Have students become bears for a day. A bear shape is provided on page 36 for a bulletin board, class book, or any of the bear activities listed in the unit.

- Read and compare several different versions of *Goldilocks and the Three Bears*. Talk about how folktales may have different versions, but certain key elements and phrases remain the same. Some good stories to try are *Goldilocks and the Three Bears* retold by James Marshall, TCM550 — *Big Book of Favorite Tales: Goldilocks and the Three Bears*, and *When Goldilocks Went to the House of the Bears* illustrated by Jenny Randall (see bibliography, page 43). After reading several versions, dramatize this classic tale.

Teddy Bear Shape

See page 35 for suggestions.

Teddy Bear Mask

See page 35 for suggestions.

Oh, What a Thanksgiving!

Author: Steven Kroll

Publisher: Scholastic, 1988

Summary: A young boy named David uses his imagination to find out what it would have been like if he could have been at the first Thanksgiving feast.

Related Holiday: Thanksgiving has been celebrated as a national holiday in the United States since 1863. It is held on the last Thursday in November as a reminder of the first Thanksgiving celebrated in 1621.

Related Poetry: "Thanksgiving" by Myra Cohn Livingston, *Celebrations* (Scholastic, 1985); *It's Thanksgiving* by Jack Prelutsky (Scholastic, 1982)

Related Songs: "Hurray, It's Thanksgiving Day!" by Jean Warren and "Thanksgiving Day Thanks" by Patricia Coyne, *Holiday Piggyback Songs* (Warren Publishing House, Inc., 1988)

Connecting Activities:

- Before reading the story, discuss with students facts that they know about the first Thanksgiving. Compare our present day Thanksgiving with the first Thanksgiving celebration. How has Thanksgiving changed? How has it remained the same?

- After reading the story, make some comparison charts to review certain elements found in the plot. To make the posters, draw a line down the center of three 12" x 18" (30 cm x 45 cm) pieces of white construction paper or tag board. Compare the *Mayflower* and the bus, the cottage and David's house, the hunting trip and the shopping trip. Make a list of similarities and differences.

- Food is an important part of every Thanksgiving celebration. Ask the students what types of foods they enjoy on Thanksgiving day. Then find out what the Pilgrims and Native Americans had to eat. Some good factual references are *The Pilgrim's First Thanksgiving* by Ann McGovern and *Sarah Morton's Day: A Day in the Life of a Pilgrim Girl* by Kate Waters (see bibliography, page 43). Fold some 9" x 12" (23 cm x 46 cm) pieces of light colored construction paper in half to make menus. List and illustrate a menu for the first Thanksgiving. Do the same for a modern day menu. Encourage the students to add lots of details in their description of the foods and the pictures. Show some real restaurant menus to help in designing the Thanksgiving menus. For example, one entree for the Pilgrim's menu might read: Classic Cornbread- delicious homemade bread baked the old-fashioned way.

- Teach the students the poem "Oh, What a Feast!" on page 41, and have them draw their own delicious Thanksgiving dinner on the plate on page 40.

Oh, What a Thanksgiving! (cont.)

- Cut out large letters approximately 15" (38 cm) tall out of tag board or construction paper. Spell the word Thanksgiving or November. Divide the class into partners or small groups and distribute the letters. For each letter, the students need to think of a theme that relates to the Thanksgiving season. The letters are then decorated with cut out pictures made from construction paper. For example, the letters might be decorated with paper turkeys, Pilgrims, feathers, or colorful fall leaves.

- For a colorful bulletin board that also enhances self-esteem, first put up a large paper turkey in your classroom, without the tail feathers. Explain to the class that in November you are launching a special project called "Feathers for Fred." Fred the turkey has lost all of his tail feathers and needs to grow some more before Thanksgiving. The children can help Fred regain feathers for his tail by following classroom rules, completing work, being a good friend, or whatever criteria is set up. In order for each child to feel a part of the activity, give each student the same number of feathers. It is then the teacher's job to catch each student being good and to give a boost of self-esteem while awarding the feathers. A positive comment can be written on the feathers which can then be taken home at the end of the month as part of a Native American headband.

- To further emphasize a spirit of cooperation and good behavior, fill out a "Thankful Certificate" for each student (page 42). The teacher completes the award by filling in the page with a comment such as "I am thankful that you were a good friend" or "I am thankful that your work showed improvement." The certificates are awarded at the end of the month and could be presented as part of a classroom feast (see next activity).

- Make pilgrim hats and Native American headbands and have your students pretend that they are at the first Thanksgiving feast. Work with your children to cook some traditional foods such as pumpkin pie, cornbread, homemade butter, and cranberry sauce (even a turkey with stuffing!). Or, enlist the help of parents by asking for donations of some healthy snacks (popcorn, raisins, etc.) to share as part of your feast. Do a class picture graph to find out what the favorite food was at the feast.

- The first Thanksgiving was characterized by a spirit of sharing and cooperation. Encourage those feelings in your students by helping others during the Thanksgiving season. You might donate some of the foods your class bakes to an agency that helps the homeless in your community. Or, hold a bake sale and use the money collected to buy a turkey to give to a needy family. Many agencies have lists of people who are "adopted" for the holidays and are provided with all the food necessary for a Thanksgiving dinner. Organize a canned food drive in your school, and collect donations in paper bags during the first two weeks of November.

Oh, What a Feast!

See page 38 for directions.

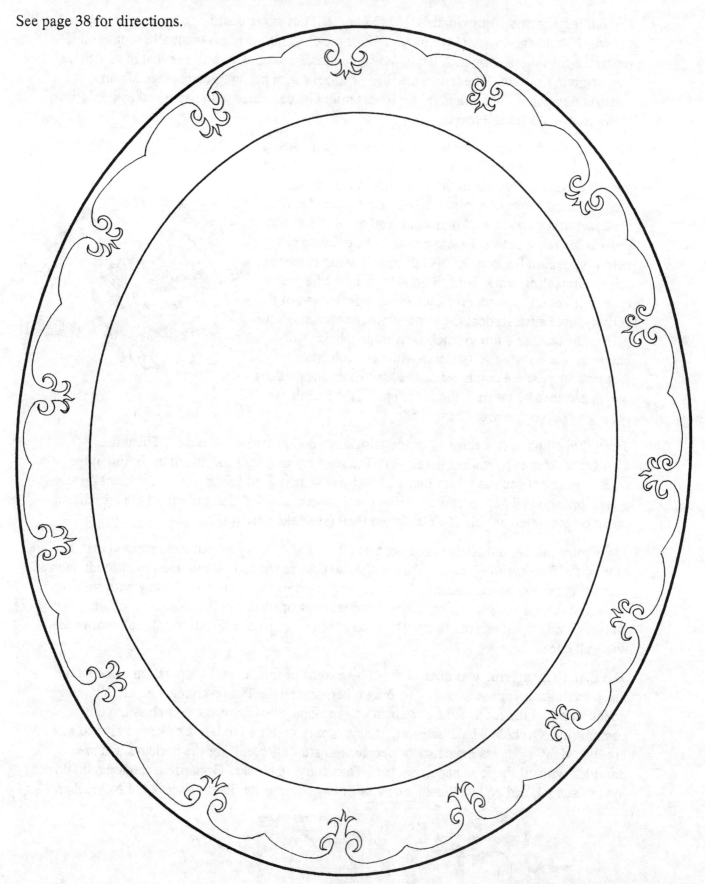

Oh, What a Feast!

by Deborah P. Cerbus

Turkey and gravy

Corn on my plate.

Oh, what a feast for me.

Cranberries and stuffing

I can't wait.

Oh, what a feast for me.

Bread and potatoes

Dessert is great.

Oh, what a feast for me.

I love Thanksgiving

Fill up my plate.

Oh, what a feast for me!

Thankful Certificate

I am thankful that _____
                                                    Student's Name

_____

_____

_____   _____
Date   *Teacher's Signature*

Thankful Certificate

I am thankful that _____
                                                    Student's Name

_____

_____

_____   _____
Date   *Teacher's Signature*

Festive Fall Bibliography

Asch, Frank. *Popcorn* (Parent's Magazine Press, 1979)

Baer, Edith. *This is the Way We Go to School: A Book About Children Around the World* (Scholastic, 1990)

Balestrino, Phillip. *The Skeleton Inside You* (Harper & Row, 1989)

Balian, Lorna. *Humbug Witch* (Humbug Press, 1965)

Barth, Edna. *Turkeys, Pilgrims, and Indian Corn: The Story of the Thanksgiving Symbols* (Clarion Books, 1975)

Bialosky, Peggy & Alan. *The Teddy Bear Catalog* (Workman Publishing, 1980)

Bridwell, Norman. *Clifford's Halloween* (Scholastic, 1966)

Brown, Marc. *Arthur's Halloween* (Little, Brown & Company, 1982)

Brown, Ruth. *A Dark Dark Tale* (Dial Books for Young Readers, 1983)

Bunting, Eve. *Scary, Scary Halloween* (Clarion Books, 1986)

Carlson, Nancy. *Harriet's Halloween Candy* (Puffin Books, 1982)

Cole, Joanna. *The Magic School Bus Inside the Human Body* (Scholastic, 1989)

Cowley, Joy. *A Monster Sandwich* (Wright Group, 1983)

DK Direct Limited. *What's Inside My Body?* (Dorling Kindersley, Inc., 1991)

Dalgliesh, Alice. *The Thanksgiving Story* (Charles Scribner's Sons, 1954)

Devlin, Wende & Harry. *Cranberry Thanksgiving* (Macmillan, 1971)

Gellman, Ellie. *It's Rosh Hashanah!* (Karben, 1985)

Gibbons, Gail. *Thanksgiving Day* (Holiday House, 1983)

Greene, Carol. *The Pilgrims are Marching: A Sing-Along Holiday Story* (Childrens Press, 1988)

Greene, Carol. *The Thirteen Days of Halloween: A Sing-Along Story* (Childrens Press, 1983)

Greenfield, Eloise. *Grandpa's Face* (Philomel Books, 1988)

Gross, Ruth Belov. *A Book About Christopher Columbus* (Scholastic, 1974)

Gross, Ruth Belov. *A Book About Your Skeleton* (Scholastic, 1978)

Hayward, Linda. *The First Thanksgiving* (Random House, 1990)

Hopkins, Lee Bennett. *Good Books, Good Times!* (Harper Collins, 1990)

Krensky, Stephen. *Christopher Columbus* (Random House, 1991)

Marshall, James. *Goldilocks and the Three Bears* (Dial Books, 1988)

McFarlan, Donald, Ed. *Guiness Book of Records* (Bantam Books, 1992)

McGovern, Ann. *If You Sailed on the Mayflower in 1620* (Scholastic, 1991)

McGovern, Ann. *The Pilgrim's First Thanksgiving* (Scholastic, 1973)

Melser, June and Joy Cowley. *In a Dark, Dark Wood* (Wright Group, 1980)

Miller, Edna. *Mousekin's Golden House* (Prentice-Hall, 1964)

Miller, Edna. *Mousekin's Thanksgiving* (Simon & Schuster, 1985)

Morris, Ann. *Bread Bread Bread* (Lothrop, Lee & Shepard, 1989)

Pelham, David. *Sam's Sandwich* (Dutton Childrens Books, 1991)

Prelutsky, Jack. *It's Thanksgiving* (Greenwillow Books, 1982)

Randall, Jenny. *When Goldilocks Went to the House of the Bears* (Scholstic, 1986)

Scott, Geoffrey. *Labor Day* (Carolrhoda Books, 1982)

Smith, Barry. *The First Voyage of Christopher Columbus, 1492* (Penguin Books, 1992)

Titherington, Jeanne. *Pumpkin, Pumpkin* (Greenwillow Books, 1986)

Waters, Kate. *Sarah Morton's Day: A Day in the Life of a Pilgrim Girl* (Scholstic, 1989)

Hanukkah!

Author: Roni Schotter

Publisher: Joy Street/Little, Brown & Company, 1990

Summary: This delightfully illustrated book tells the story of a modern-day family's celebration of Hanukkah and the joy it brings to the family, especially the young children.

Related Holiday: Hanukkah, or the Festival of Lights, has been celebrated by Jewish people around the world for 2000 years. It lasts for eight days and comes at the end of November or in December. Hanukkah is a holiday to celebrate the victory of Judah Maccabee over King Antiochus for the right to worship their own God. When the Jewish people won the battle, they celebrated for eight days. Although only enough oil to light the menorah for one day was found, the oil burned for eight days.

Related Poetry: "Hanukkah Candles" by Jean Warren, *Small World Celebrations* (Warren Publishing House, 1988)

Related Songs: "Hanukkah, Hanukkah" by Carla C. Skjong, "Eight Little Candles" by Jean Warren, and "I'm a Little Dreidel" (adapted traditional), *Holiday Piggyback Songs* (Warren Publishing House, 1988)

Connecting Activities:

*   To build your students' knowledge about Hanukkah, plan to read (or have available for students' independent reading) several factual books about this holiday, such as *My First Chanukah* by Tomie dePaola, *A Picture Book of Hanukkah* by David A. Adler, *All About Hanukkah* by Judye Groner and Madeline Wikler, and *Latkes and Applesauce* by Fran Manushkin (see bibliography, page 93).

*   Invite a guest speaker to come into your classroom to explain the history of Hanukkah and how Hanukkah is celebrated in his or her home. Perhaps some of your students could share their experiences in celebrating Hanukkah.

*   List with your students the ways that the family in *Hanukkah!* celebrated the holiday. Be sure to include lighting the menorah, eating latkes, playing dreidel (dray dl) games, and giving gifts.

*   During the story, the older boy teaches his younger brother to "Hanukkah" correctly. Help students to learn the correct pronunciation (hon oo kah).

*   Encourage your students to make their own special signs for Hanukkah similar to the one in the story that the young girl made. Save these to display on the "Happy Hanukkah" bulletin board described on the next page.

Hanukkah! (cont.)

- The last two pages of *Hanukkah!* give a useful summary of the story of Hanukkah and words which are unique to this celebration. Explain the significance of the menorah and the shamash to Hanukkah. Bring in a real menorah and shamash to share with your students and to illustrate the lighting of the menorah.

- Make a large menorah (candle holder with nine branches) on a ''Happy Hanukkah'' bulletin board as the center of your Hanukkah celebration. Use bright blue paper for the background, and gold foil wrapping paper cut into the shape of the menorah. Use cardboard paper towel tubes covered with white or colorful paper for the candles. Attach a yellow construction paper flame at the top of each candle. Place the shamash (helper candle) a little higher than the other candles and in the center of the menorah. Add another candle to the menorah each day during the eight days of your celebration.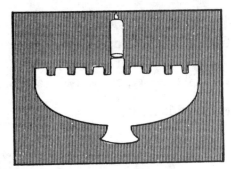

- Purchase plastic dreidels for each student or make dreidels using the directions on page 46. Explain the basic game to your students. Play dreidel games in small groups.

- Introduce your students to Hanukkah gelt (money) by giving them chocolate coins wrapped in gold paper as one kind of gift which children receive during Hanukkah. During Hanukkah, gifts may be given each night, or sometimes just on the last night. Chocolate Hanukkah gelt would be a fun souvenir for each student.

- Challenge your students to make a Class Chart to compare and contrast Hanukkah, Christmas, and Kwanzaa. Children should notice that all involve gift-giving and feasting and all three celebrations fall within the same months. As to the differences, children should consider the length, the dates, traditional foods, and the history of each celebration.

- Make latkes, the traditional potato pancakes fried in oil, which are served during Hanukkah. The oil is used to remember the oil that burned for eight days instead of one. A recipe for latkes may be found in *Latkes and Applesauce* by Fran Manushkin (Scholastic, 1990).

- Applesauce is the traditional complement for latkes. Make some homemade applesauce to enjoy with your latkes during the final day of your Hanukkah celebration.

The Dreidel Game

Directions: Cut out the dreidel. Make holes as shown below. Fold along the inside lines to make a box. Fold the tabs inward. Use glue or tape to hold the dreidel together. Push a pencil or pen through the holes. Spin the dreidel and begin play.

To Play the Game

The dreidel is a four-sided spinning top. The letters written on the side of the dreidel are Hebrew for "A Great Miracle Happened Here." Each symbol represents a different instruction for the game. To play, give each person a designated number of markers (gelt, candy, nuts, etc.). Each player puts one marker in the center, or "kitty," each time the dreidel is spun. Players take turns spinning the dreidel.

If the dreidel lands on:

nun	gimmel	hay	shin
The player does nothing.	The player receives the whole kitty.	The player receives half of the kitty.	The player must put one marker in the kitty.

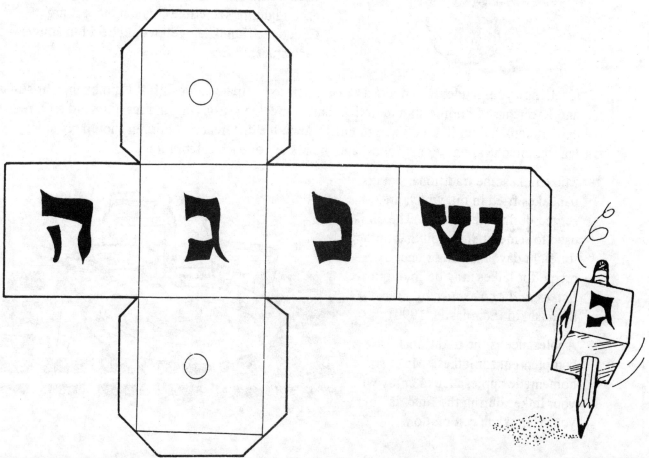

Christmas Tree Memories

Author: Aliki

Publisher: Harper Collins, 1991

Summary: This beautifully illustrated book tells the story of two children and their parents as they share memories around the Christmas tree on Christmas Eve.

Related Holiday: Christmas Eve is a Christian celebration on the night of December 24th to observe the eve of the birth of Jesus Christ.

Related Poetry: "It's Christmas" and "Our Christmas Tree" by Jack Prelutsky, *It's Christmas* (Greenwillow, 1981); "In the Week When Christmas Comes" by Eleanor Farjeon, "Day Before Christmas" by Marchette Chute, "A Visit from St. Nicholas" by Clement Clarke Moore, and "A Merry Literary Christmas" by Alice Low, *The Family Read-Aloud Christmas Treasury* (Little, Brown & Company, 1989)

Related Songs: Traditional songs "Deck the Halls," "Jingle Bells", "Petit Papa Noel" by Henri Martinet and Raymond Vinci, "Every Little Wish" by Raffi, "Douglas Mountain" by Arnold Sundgaard and Alec Wilder, and "Christmas Time's a Coming" by Tex Logan, *The Raffi Christmas Treasury* (Crown, 1988); traditional songs from *Wee Sing for Christmas* (Price/Stern/Sloan, 1984)

Connecting Activities:

- After reading *Christmas Tree Memories* to your class, make a list of all of the ornaments which were shown in the book on a large ornament shape. Then have your class make some of their favorites from the book (dough hearts, pine cone angels, origami shapes, etc.), which could serve as your guide in making these ornaments. Discuss the special memories they are making as they create their own handmade ornaments. (If your school has a school Christmas tree, select some of your students' handmade ornaments to display on this special tree for the entire school to enjoy.)

- Have your students make simple tree-shaped ornaments from two 6" x 9" (15 cm x 23 cm) pieces of green construction paper. Stuff the two shapes with a scrap of newspaper. Stitch the two tree shapes together using colorful yarn. Have the students glue a photograph of themselves at the top. Add finishing decorations with scraps of rick-rack, lace, fabric trim, and glitter to both sides of the ornament.

- Ask the children to bring in a favorite non-breakable ornament from home. Children then tell why the ornament is special to them. The ornaments could be sorted into groups such as "Made With Paper," "Made With Beads," "Made With Clay," etc.

Christmas Tree Memories *(cont.)*

- Enlist the aid of parents by sending a note to them asking them to briefly describe a family tradition which is special to them. These traditions could be typed or handwritten and illustrated by your students and then duplicated to make books with a suitable title (such as "Our Christmas Memories") for each of your students to take home.

- Try one or both of these graph ideas with your students.

  — Make a large Christmas tree shape from green tag board. Make a graph with three columns on the shape. Label one column "Real," another column "Artificial," and the last column "No Tree." Laminate the graph. Give each of your students a colorful Christmas sticker to put in the column that identifies his or her tree for Christmas.

  — Make a class graph of favorite "Tree Toppers." Make a different laminated tree for each of the three tree topper choices on your graph: angel, star, bell. Children sign their name with a wipe off pen on the tree of their choice. Display the graph.

- If possible, take your class on a field trip to a Christmas tree lot or a public horticulture garden to learn about the life of a Christmas tree. For starters, find out how the trees are grown, how Christmas trees came to be included in the Christmas celebration, the types of trees that are grown as Christmas trees, how they are shaped, and how many trees are needed each year as Christmas trees. Display field trip photographs and a group dictated story about the trip on a bulletin board in your classroom. If a trip is not possible, read the factual book *Christmas Trees* by Kathy Henderson (see bibliography, page 93) to your class to learn about real Christmas trees.

- Try growing some evergreen tree seedlings in your classroom during the winter season. When spring comes, they could be planted outside in the yard of your school (perhaps on Arbor Day in your area). Keep a record of the growth of your trees.

- Read the delightful classic *Mr. Willowby's Christmas Tree* by Robert Barry (see bibliography, page 93) to your class. Have students make a story map and a class Big Book of its events. This book could also begin a discussion of fractions and recycling.

- Have your students make three-dimensional trees. Give each of your students two large 18" x 24" (46 cm x 61 cm) sheets of green construction paper. Children trace around a large Christmas tree shape pattern on each of the two sheets. Use tempera paint to decorate one side of each of the trees. When the paint is dry, both trees are cut out, stuffed with newspaper, and stapled around the edges. Hang trees from the ceiling for a forest effect.

- Have each of the students in your class (and all of the students and staff in the school) trace around their hands, with fingers outstretched, on green construction paper. Cut out the hand prints carefully. Curl hand prints by rolling the fingers around a pencil. Decorate by designing colorful ornaments on the palms of the hand prints. Create a giant tree shape by pointing the hand prints down and gluing them onto a large piece of butcher paper or stapling them to a bulletin board. Display in a large room or lobby of the school.

Christmas Tree Memories *(cont.)*

- Encourage your students to begin a tradition at home. Duplicate the classic poem "A Visit from St. Nicholas" by Clement C. Moore in groups of four or eight lines per page. Have the students create their own illustrations. Practice choral reading and illustrate one page of the poem each day (review previous days' pages each successive day). With repetition many students will have memorized most of the poem, so that when it goes home as a special gift for the student's family the student will be able to lead a Christmas Eve family reading of the poem.

- Expand your students' knowledge of Christmas traditions and customs by reading *Christmas Around the World* by Emily Kelley (see bibliography, page 93), which mentions customs from Mexico, Iran, China, Sweden, Iraq, Spain, Norway, Australia, New Zealand, France, and Germany. Use a world map posted on a bulletin board to locate the countries for which customs are identified in the book. List the customs and traditions on the world map in the correct locations. Add them to the bulletin board. Add signs around the world map that say "Merry Christmas" in a variety of foreign languages (some are listed below).

Danish — *Glaedelig Jul*

Finnish — *Hauskaa Joulua*

French — *Joyeux Noël*

German — *Fröhliche Weinachten*

Greek — *Kala Christougenna*

Italian — *Buon Natale*

Norwegian/Swedish — *God Jul*

Portuguese — *Feliz Natal*

Russian — *S Rozhdyestvom Khristovym*

Spanish — *Feliz Navidad*

- Using the child shape on page 50, have students add native costumes to represent one of these countries. Make a speech bubble for the child saying "Merry Christmas" in the appropriate language.

- Hold a "Christmas Around the World Pageant" where students present their knowledge of Christmas traditions and customs from around the world to other classrooms and parents. Children may wear simple costumes or carry simple props to dramatize the various traditions and customs. Be sure to include foods, Christmas cookies, seasonal songs, and games from around the world.

Merry Christmas from Around the World

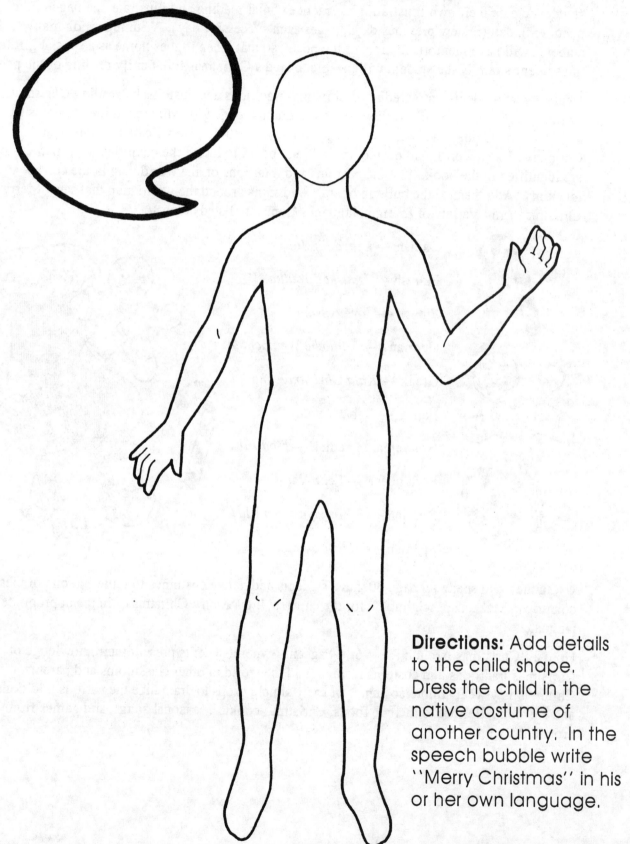

Directions: Add details to the child shape. Dress the child in the native costume of another country. In the speech bubble write "Merry Christmas" in his or her own language.

The Polar Express

Author: Chris Van Allsburg

Publisher: Houghton Mifflin, 1985

Summary: This Caldecott medal winner tells the story of a special train ride that takes a young boy on a trip to the North Pole to receive the first gift of Christmas from Santa Claus.

Related Holiday: Christmas is a Christian holiday celebrated around the world on December 25th to celebrate the birth of Jesus Christ.

Related Poetry: ''Dear Santa Claus'' and ''Another Santa Claus'' by Jack Prelutsky, *It's Christmas* (Greenwillow, 1981); ''Christmas Eve'' by David McCord, ''A Visit from St. Nicholas'' by Clement Clarke Moore, and ''The Joy of Giving'' by John Greenleaf Whittier, *The Family Read-Aloud Christmas Treasury* (Little, Brown & Company, 1989)

Related Songs: ''Must Be Santa'' by Hal Moore and Bill Fredicks and ''Jolly Old Saint Nicholas'' (U.S.A.), *Wee Sing for Christmas* (Price/Stern/Sloan, 1984); ''Up on the Housetop'' (traditional) and ''On Christmas Morning'' by Chris Whiteley and Raffi, *The Raffi Christmas Treasury* (Crown Publishers, 1988)

Connecting Activities:

- Prior to reading or showing *The Polar Express* to your class, wrap a small box in festive wrapping paper as a present for your class and have students brainstorm a list of ideas of what might be inside the box. Introduce the book to the class and discuss what the book might be about. Give each child a ticket for boarding the Polar Express (see page 53 for tickets and an extension activity using money).

- While you read *The Polar Express* to your class, wear a conductor's hat and punch each child's ticket with a hole punch as the children come aboard the train to listen to the story.

- Immediately after reading *The Polar Express* to your class, give each child a small gold bell strung on a length of narrow red ribbon as a story keepsake. This is what was given to the boy who truly believed.

- Have the children discuss what they would have asked to receive from Santa Claus as the first gift of Christmas. List their choices on a large chart. Try to sort and classify their choices into groups (toys, reindeer items, gifts for the world, etc.).

The Polar Express *(cont.)*

- Make a Polar Express bulletin board. Have the children write original Christmas stories on train car shapes. Make a train engine and caboose for your train and add a title such as "The First Grade Writing Express."

- Use the North Pole Express Game Board on pages 55 and 56 to help students retell the story. You may choose to color the game board and laminate it before placing it in a Polar Express Learning Center. Adapt the open spaces to fit your class needs (math facts, sight words, etc.). In order to play, you will need a die and markers (beans, pennies, seeds, plastic discs, etc.) for each group of 2-4 players. Have players roll a die to determine the number of boxes to move along the game board, following directions as they proceed. The winner is the first player to reach Santa's Castle.

- Discuss real trains with your students. Assess their prior knowledge by making a list of facts that they can tell you about trains. Read about real trains. Compare a steam engine with an electric engine. Set up a toy train in the classroom. Visit a real railroad station, if possible.

- Create a Christmas math learning center. Provide a variety of items such as small bells, candy canes, a bag of bows, red and green jellybeans, and holiday candy. Use the items for estimation activities by putting them into seasonal-shaped jars such as hollow candy canes, glass Christmas tree jars, or glass candy jars. Children may write their estimates on laminated cardboard Christmas decorations with a washable marker.

- Have each student bring in a non-breakable Christmas item to be used for sorting and classifying. Make labels for your categories such as "sweet and tasty," "decorative," or "green."

- Keep classroom Christmas picture books in a large Santa's sack that can be made and labeled using a large green garbage bag. Add this to your Polar Express Learning Center to give the "gift of reading" to your students.

- Have your students give the "gift of poetry." Fold a piece of 9" x 12" (23 cm x 30 cm) white construction paper in half. Children use red paint to make a bow on the top (the folded edge) of the white rectangle, which is now a gift box card. On the inside of the gift box, have children create their own Christmas poem or cinquain (or print a favorite published poem). These cards could also be used to write thank-you notes to relatives and friends for their holiday gifts.

- Conduct a study of the polar region. Find the North Pole on a globe. Discuss the animals that are native to this region. Read a variety of books about this region such as *The Wild Christmas Reindeer* by Jan Brett, *White Bear, Ice Bear* by Joanne Ryder, and *Nessa's Fish* by Nancy Luenn (see bibliography, page 93). Create a "Polar Bear Express Center" at which students may do research about the region. Paint a large box to use as a cave or igloo for your children to climb into to read about this region.

- Have your students pretend that they are going on a trip to the North Pole. Have them determine how they would get there and how long the trip would be. Map out their route on a real map, and record what they would see on their trip in a "Polar Bear Express Journal."

Tickets Please

The boy in *The Polar Express* doesn't seem to need a ticket to get on the train. If we were to go on a train would we need a ticket? Provide each student with at least two copies of the tickets below, a pencil, and the coins provided on page 54 (real coins can be used as well).

Directions: Let the children fill in their names and the cost of the ticket. For young children keep the cost below five cents. Older children can work with nickels, dimes, and quarters so you may charge more for the tickets. After the children have filled out the tickets with their names and the price, they will need to place the appropriate number of coins on their tickets. Have students check each other's prices and coins. Trade tickets and buy your partner's ticket. Trade with another child and buy that ticket.

POLAR EXPRESS TICKET

This is a ticket to the North Pole. Use this ticket for a magical ride on the Polar Express.

This ticket belongs to _____ .

Ticket Cost: _____

POLAR EXPRESS TICKET

This is a ticket to the North Pole. Use this ticket for a magical ride on the Polar Express.

This ticket belongs to _____ .

Ticket Cost: _____

POLAR EXPRESS TICKET

This is a ticket to the North Pole. Use this ticket for a magical ride on the Polar Express.

This ticket belongs to _____ .

Ticket Cost: _____

Coins

Use with page 53.

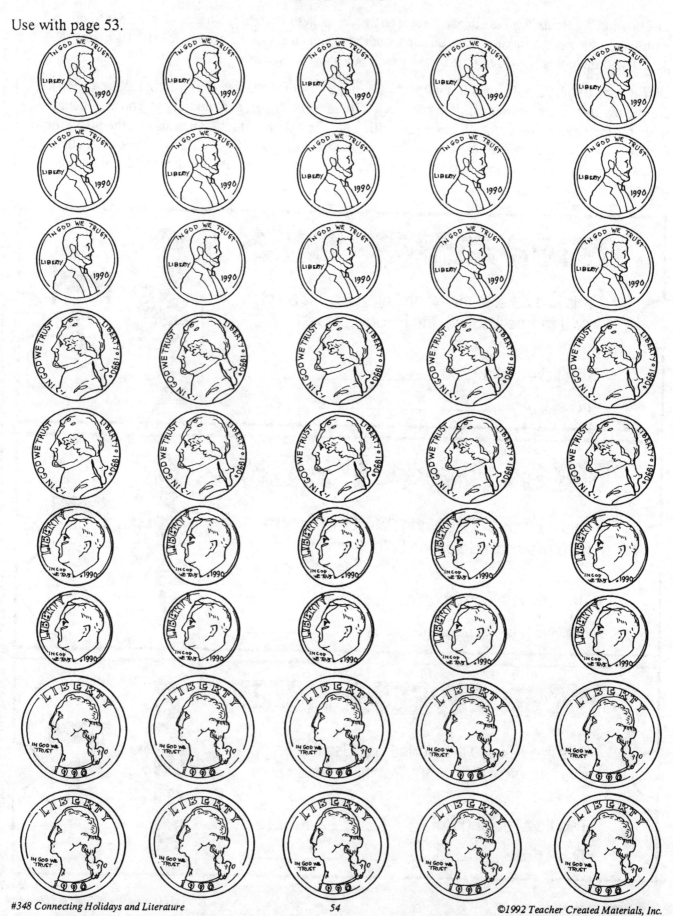

North Pole Express

See page 52 for directions.

Gift Box

Take another turn.

Climb on Board

Avalanche

Lose one turn.

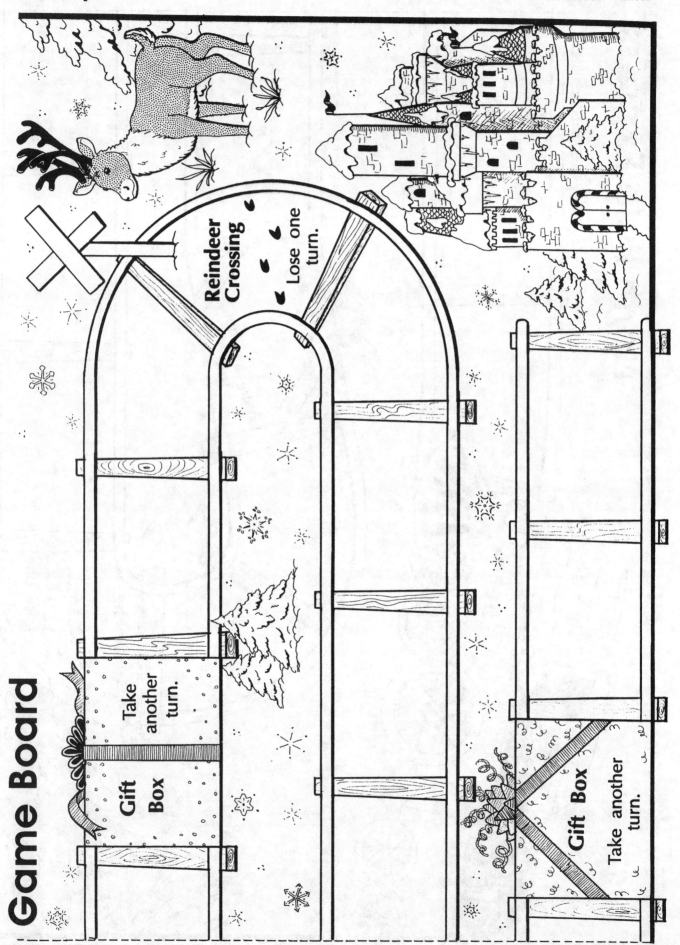

Game Board

Reindeer Crossing

Lose one turn.

Gift Box — Take another turn.

Gift Box — Take another turn.

Kwanzaa

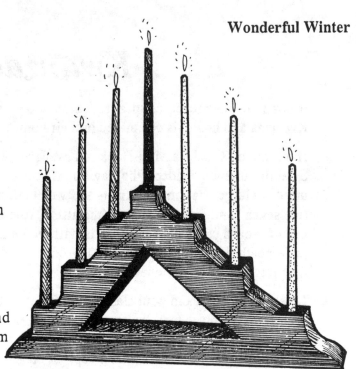

Author: A. P. Porter

Publisher: Carolrhoda Books, Inc., 1991

Summary: Through its expository text, this book tells about the African-American holiday devoted to teaching about Africa and the African culture, as well as the history and future of African-Americans.

Related Holiday: Kwanzaa is an African-American holiday created by Maulana Karenga in 1966 to honor African-Americans and their history. Kwanzaa lasts for seven days, from December 26 until January 1.

Related Poetry: ''Kwanzaa Candles'' by Elizabeth McKinnon, *Small World Celebrations* (Warren Publishing House, 1988)

Related Songs: ''Kwanzaa's Here'' by Jean Warren, *Small World Celebrations* (Warren Publishing House, 1988)

Connecting Activities:

- Since this is a relatively new holiday, you might want to build a library of other good resource books about Kwanzaa, such as *Kwanzaa* by Deborah M. Newton Chocolate and *Imani's Gift at Kwanzaa* by Denise Burden-Patmon (see bibliography, page 93).

- Discuss with your students the fact that Kwanzaa is an African-American celebration beginning the day after Christmas and continuing until January 1. ''Kwanzaa'' is an east African Swahili word meaning ''the first.'' For centuries, Africans celebrated the harvest of the first crops. Now Kwanzaa is a time for thanksgiving. To build students' knowledge of Kwanzaa, ask if they have ever been to a family reunion or a large family gathering and what they did there. Have your students listen to learn how Kwanzaa is like Thanksgiving or a family reunion. Is it similar to Christmas or Hanukkah? How?

- Discuss African-American history with your students. Help your students to learn about famous African-Americans, especially the people mentioned in the the text and illustrations in the books you read to your class about Kwanzaa (Harriet Tubman, Sojourner Truth, and Dr. Martin Luther King, Jr.). You might refer to the mini-book on pages 69-71 for information about famous African-Americans or the section about Dr. Martin Luther King, Jr. on pages 67-71.

- Children may paint their own bendera flags. Use an 18" x 24" (46 cm x 61 cm) piece of white construction paper for each flag. Children may use red, black, and green tempera paint to make their flags. Explain that the flag's three colors represent important concepts: red for the struggle for fairness and freedom, black for black people staying together, and green for the future. Have a sample for your students to view as they make their flags.

Kwanzaa (cont.)

- If possible, have resource speakers come into your classroom to explain the significance of Kwanzaa and how it is celebrated in their homes.

- Have students make a Mini-Book of Kwanzaa. Many of the Kwanzaa words come from Swahili. Include bendera (the flag for African-Americans), mkeka (place mat), kikombe cha umoja (a large cup), mazao (fruits and vegetables), kinara (the candle holder), mishumaa saba (the seven candles), and zawadi (the gifts). Run copies of pages 59-60 back-to-back. Make a copy for each child. Cut the page in half on the dashed line. Place the bottom half (pages 6, 3) underneath the top half (pages 8, 1). Fold along the solid line and staple. Have students color in the pictures and read the text.

- Celebrate Kwanzaa in your classroom. Create a Kwanzaa Corner. Collect the seven symbols of Kwanzaa: the place mat, the cup, fruits and vegetables, a candle holder for seven candles, seven candles (one black, three red, and three green), corn, and simple gifts (books and handmade gifts). Also have a bendera and a copy of the seven reasons for Kwanzaa (goals for which African-Americans are to strive), called the nguzo saba.

- Make a bulletin board of the nguzo saba, the seven principles for Kwanzaa (see *Kwanzaa*, pages 54 - 55). Since many homes put a copy of the nguzo saba on the wall during Kwanzaa, divide your bulletin board into seven equal parts, devoting one part to each of the seven principles. Have students use words and illustrations to represent each to the principles, indicating which candle in the kinara will be lit for that principle.

- Celebrate Kwanzaa in your classroom over a seven day period. (Since holiday vacation may interfere, you may need to alter your celebration dates.) Using the Kwanzaa books as a guide to your celebration, discuss the correct one of the seven principles on each day (Umoja- unity, Kujichagulia- self-determination, Ujima- collective work and responsibility, Ujamaa- cooperative economics, Nia- purpose, Kuumba- creativity, Imani- faith).

- Have a feast (karamu) on the sixth day of your celebration. Place a large mkeka (place mat) on the floor. Put a kikombe (a large cup) on the mkeka. Put the mazao (fruits and vegetables), such as apples, potatoes, fruit salad, bananas, and oranges, on the mkeka. Put one ear of corn on the mkeka for each child. Place the kinara (candle holder) in the center of the mkeka. Enjoy the mazao and perhaps serve apple juice, too. On the final day, give each of your students a simple gift (zawadi). A handmade bookmark to serve as a souvenir of Kwanzaa would be suitable.

- Do some research about African musical instruments. Play a recording of African music for your students. Bring in a variety of instruments (such as drums and flutes). Children may make their own African drums from oatmeal boxes and use these to make their own music during the feast.

Mini-Book

See page 58 for directions.

The zawadi are the gifts given to the children.

8

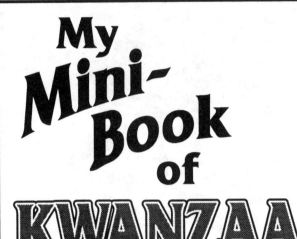

My Mini-Book of KWANZAA

By _____

1

The mazao are the fruits and vegetables put on the mkeka. The mazao stand for all work.

6

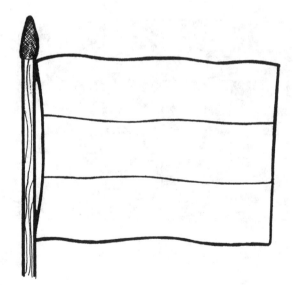

The bendera is the flag created to honor African-Americans.

3

Mini-Book *(cont.)*

See page 58 for directions.

Kwanzaa is an African-American Holiday that lasts from December 26 to January 1. It honors black people and their history.

2

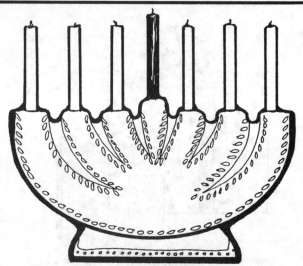

The kinara is the candle holder that stands for the people who lived in Africa long ago. The mishumaa saba are the seven candles in the kinara.

7

The mkeka is the first symbol of Kwanzaa. It is a place mat that stands for history.

4

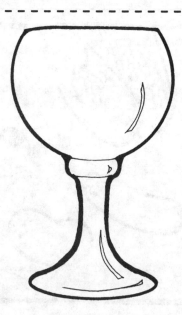

The kikombe cha umoja is a large cup that stands for staying together.

5

Happy New Year

Author: Emily Kelley

Publisher: Carolrhoda Books, 1984

Summary: This factual book describes many of the various and interesting ways the new year is celebrated around the world, sometimes on days other than January 1st.

Related Holiday: New Year's Day is a holiday that welcomes in the new year. In the United States, this celebration is on January 1st.

Related Poetry: ''New Year's Eve'' by Myra Cohn Livingston, *Celebrations* (Holiday House, 1985); ''Beginning a New Year Means'' by Ruth Whitman, ''Chinese New Year'' - a traditional Chinese nursery rhyme, and ''Bouquet of Roses'' - a traditional Puerto Rican song, *The Family Read-Aloud Holiday Treasury* (Little, Brown & Company, 1991)

Related Songs: ''A Brand New Year'' by Neoma Kreuter, ''New Year's Day'' by Sue Brown, ''Happy New Year'' by Betty Loew White, and ''A New Year on Our Calendar'' by Nancy Nason Biddinger, *Holiday Piggyback Songs* (Warren Publishing House, 1988); the traditional ''Auld Lang Syne''

Connecting Activities:

- To create a festive atmosphere when you read this book to your class, bring in a few helium filled balloons. Fasten them together with curling ribbon and make them into a balloon bouquet. Attach them to your storytime area.

- As you read the book, record the name of each country mentioned (after locating it on the classroom globe) and the New Year's customs of that country on a colorful construction paper balloon shape. Make a different balloon (attach a ribbon to it) for each of the thirteen countries mentioned in the book. Save the balloons and display them on your classroom door, as suggested on the next page.

- Make a Comparison Chart of each country's customs. Your chart should include columns to list the name of the country, date of celebration, length of celebration, name of celebration, special foods, and special customs. Display this chart in a New Year's Center. At this center you might also include a table on which you and your students may display a variety of items which are mentioned in the book as being a part of the celebrations from around the world (a scarecrow, colored eggs, pine branches, bamboo, flowers, etc.).

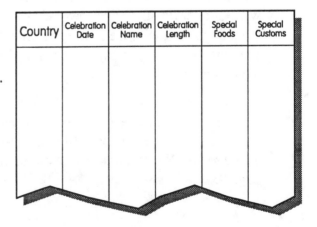

Country	Celebration Date	Celebration Name	Celebration Length	Special Foods	Special Customs

Happy New Year (cont.)

- Use the classroom globe and/or world map to discuss what continents are, the names of the seven continents, what oceans are, and the names of the four oceans. Put together pages 64 and 65 to make world maps for your students to use with this activity. Color the continents and oceans appropriately and display these in your social studies area. (You could make a similar map-match-up using a large classroom map and including the flag for each country, too). Do a "Happy New Year Map-Match-Up" using the information cards from page 66. Students cut out and glue the cards onto the map to identify the country and its customs. (Have students glue the map onto a large piece of paper and attach the cards around the map near the matching countries.)

- Create a Classroom Door Greeting. Cover your classroom door with butcher paper. Make a banner that says "Happy New Year" in block letters or using computer graphics. Display your helium balloons from page 61 around the title. A small gift tag could be attached to the door saying "To: The Students at Our School" and "From: Around the World."

- Use a calendar of the year on which to record the names and countries of the various New Year's celebrations around the world, so that you can remember that the celebrations are not all on January 1st. When you come to a celebration date, reread that country's section of the book to your class to remember what that country does on this date.

- Discuss the Chinese New Year briefly. See pages 72-75 for specific activities about this celebration. Discuss Rosh Hashanah, the Jewish New Year, that is celebrated in the fall of the year and read *The World's Birthday: A Rosh Hashanah Story* by Barbara Diamond Goldin (see bibliography, page 93) to the class.

- To help students remember the book and share what they learned at home, give each child a story keepsake party horn, available at any party store. Instruct children to blow their horns at a signal given by you, such as when you strike the xylophone twelve times, to simulate the clock striking twelve at midnight on New Year's Eve. Discuss the customs in the book that involved making noise as one way to greet the new year.

- Discuss the concept of New Year's resolutions with your students. Have them relate something which they would like to do better or change about themselves during the new year. Cut out party hat shapes and have your students write and/ or illustrate their own resolutions on them beginning with the sentence starter "This year I'll try to..." Display these resolutions on a bulletin board.

- Perhaps one resolution for today's busy families could be to relax more often. Teachers and students alike would enjoy the book *Take Time To Relax!* by Nancy Carlson (see bibliography, page 93).

     62

Happy New Year *(cont.)*

- Since laughing on New Year's Eve is supposed to bring good luck, have your students create their own ''Class Book of Riddles.'' Each child could write his or her riddle at the top of an 8" (20 cm) square piece of paper. The answer to the riddle could be hidden under a 5" x 8" (13 cm x 20 cm) paper flap attached to the bottom 5" of the page with adhesive tape. Encourage your students to add a lot of color and details to illustrate the answers to their riddles under the flap, too. Make a cover for your class book using colorful tag board. Add a title and decorate the cover with party hats, horns, confetti, and question marks.

- Your students could create their own Happy New Year hats. Begin with a colorful sheet of 12" x 18" (30 cm x 46 cm) construction paper. Fold up a two-inch strip along the bottom of the paper to make a brim for your hat. Staple the paper into a cone shape. Children may write ''Happy New Year'' on the brim. Use streamers, spirals, accordion-folded paper strips, glitter, and sequins to decorate the hats. Wear these hats during the following activity.

- As a culminating activity, have a ''New Year's Brunch'' with your class. Invite your principal and other special guests (librarian, music teacher, art teacher, secretary, custodian, etc.). Serve the following foods, all of which are mentioned in the book: pancakes (France), grapes (Spain), eggs and rice pilaf (Iran), and English wassail (recipe in the book). For entertainment during your brunch, sing some of the songs listed in the unit, recite listed poems, tell about various customs and identify their countries or origin, explain your classroom displays, and tell a few of your class riddles.

Happy New Year

See page 62 for directions.

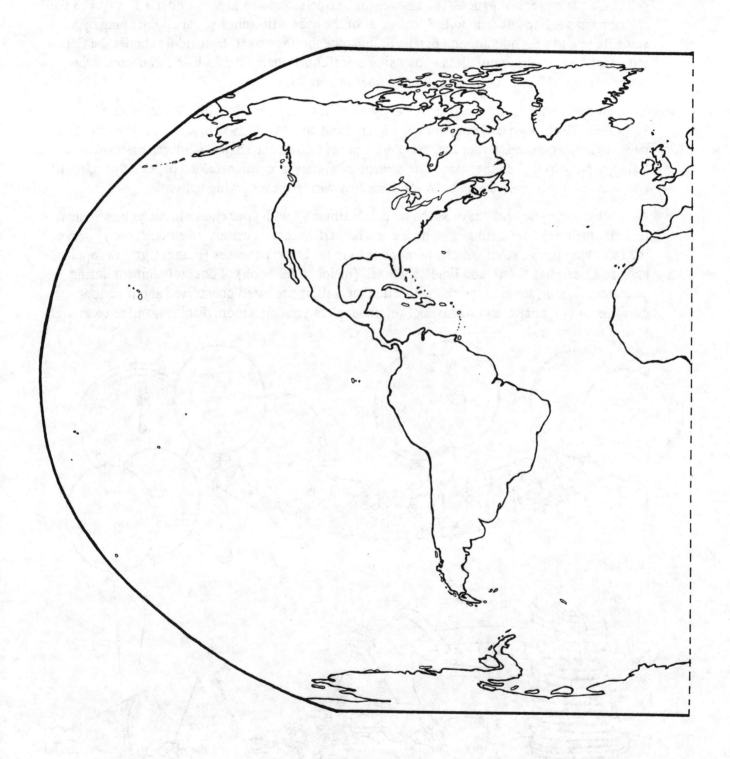

Map Match-Up

Map Match-Up Cards

Directions: Cut out these cards. Glue them near the correct country on your map (pages 64-65) and draw a line to the country named on the card.

In Spain, people eat twelve grapes for good luck at midnight on New Year's Eve.	In Greece, St. Basil fills children's shoes with presents on New Year's Eve.
In Puerto Rico, children throw pails of water out of their windows at midnight on New Year's Eve.	In Japan, people begin to laugh and laugh when the New Year arrives. It is believed to bring them good luck all year.
In France, people have pancakes on New Year's Day for good luck all year.	In Sierra Leone, Africa, people sing, dance, and carry buckets of water on their heads to show thanks for the rain that will come.
In China, people celebrate with fireworks and a huge parade with a gigantic paper dragon.	In Equador, South America, a scarecrow becomes part of most families' celebrations.
In Iran, people eat eggs and rice pilaf every year for good luck.	In Belgium, farmers wish their animals a Happy New Year.

What Is Martin Luther King, Jr. Day?

Author: Margot Parker

Publisher: Childrens Press, 1990

Summary: The fictional child characters in this book learn of the importance of Dr. Martin Luther King, Jr., as well as the story of his life, through factual information and real photographs.

Related Holiday: Martin Luther King, Jr. Day is celebrated throughout the United States on the third Monday of January to honor civil rights leader and Nobel Prize winner, Dr. Martin Luther King, Jr., whose real birthday was January 15, 1929.

Related Poetry: "Martin Luther King Day" by Myra Cohn Livingston, *Celebrations* (Holiday House, 1985); "Dreams " by Langston Hughes, *The Family Read-Aloud Holiday Treasury* (Little, Brown & Company, 1991); "Martin Luther King" by Myra Cohn Livingston, *The Random House Book of Poetry for Children* (Random House, 1983)

Related Songs: "Martin Luther King" by Josette Brown, "Brotherhood" by Debra Lindahl, and "Dr. King" by Debra Butler, *Holiday Piggyback Songs* (Warren Publishing House, 1988)

Connecting Activities:

- Before reading this book to your class, assess your students' prior knowledge by doing a K-W-L activity. List on a chart (or on a chalkboard) the facts that your students **know** about Martin Luther King, Jr. Next, ask them to tell you what they **want to know** about him as they listen to the book; add these ideas to your chart. Then read the book to your students. After they have heard the story, have your students tell you what they **learned** about him; add these facts to your chart. Your children should check their lists of what they wanted to find out about him and see if they did find out all that they wanted. If not, refer to the other books about his life, such as *A Picture Book of Martin Luther King, Jr.* by David A. Adler and *Martin Luther King Day* by Linda Lowery (see bibliography, page 93). Keep these books in a special center at which you may include commercially-made posters, articles, and other books for a "Famous African-Americans Center."

- Use Martin Luther King, Jr. Day to begin a study of African-Americans. Continue the unit through February, which is African-American history month. Have each student use pages 69-71 to create a Mini-Book of Famous African-Americans. Cut the mini-pages apart. Staple together to make a booklet. Students may put pages in alphabetical order by the person's last name.

What Is Martin Luther King, Jr. Day?

(cont.)

- Have students work in cooperative groups of two or three to make a time line called "The Life of Martin Luther King, Jr." Each group should use an 18" x 24" (46 cm x 61 cm) sheet of paper to depict one part of Dr. King's life and accomplishments. Have students, or the teacher, write one of the following sentences on each sheet of paper. The student then illustrates the sentence.

  – *Martin Luther King was born in Atlanta, Georgia on January 15, 1929.*

  – *Martin's father was a minister, and Martin liked to sing and make speeches.*

  – *Martin was a very good student.*

  – *Martin Luther King, Jr. became a minister, married, and had four children. He led peaceful marches to fight for the belief that all people should be treated equally under the law.*

  – *Dr. King gave his "I Have a Dream" speech in August of 1963 at the biggest civil rights march held in Washington, D. C.*

  – *Martin Luther King was awarded the Nobel Peace Prize.*

  – *Dr. King was assassinated in April of 1968.*

  – *Martin Luther King, Jr. Day became a national holiday in 1986 and is celebrated in many ways.*

  When all the groups have completed their pages, have the class work together to sequence them in the correct order to tell about Dr. King's life. The completed pages could be hung on a clothesline along a wall in your classroom or in a long hallway.

- Discuss Dr. King's "I Have a Dream" speech. If age-appropriate, read the speech to your class or listen to a recording of it. Brainstorm a list of ways to keep Dr. King's dream alive.

- Make a bulletin board about Dr. Martin Luther King, Jr., with the title "Dr. King's Dream." Display a poster of Dr. King in the center. Have each of your students paint a picture showing what his dream means to him or her (playing with friends of different races, shaking hands, going to school with children of many ethnic origins, etc.).

- Discuss the significance of the Nobel Peace Prize. This is awarded each year to the person who has done the most effective work in the interest of world peace. Dr. King received this medal and cash award in 1964 for leading the African-Americans' struggle for equality in the United States through non-violent methods. The text of *What Is Martin Luther King, Jr. Day?* notes that Dr. King did not keep the money, but gave it away to other people who had worked with him for peace. Award each of your students a "Peace Prize" for their work toward getting along well with others or finding peaceful solutions to conflicts (see TCM345 *Connecting Social Studies and Literature*, page 137).

Mini-Book

See page 67 for directions.

FAMOUS
African-Americans

Name _____

Dr. Martin Luther King, Jr. won the Nobel Peace Prize for working in peaceful ways to get equal rights for African-Americans.

Thurgood Marshall was the first African-American to serve on the United States Supreme Court.

Jesse Owens won four gold medals in track and field at the 1936 Olympic Games in Berlin.

Langston Hughes was a famous writer of poetry, books, plays, and songs.

Bill Cosby is a famous comedian, TV star, and movie star.

Rev. Jesse Jackson is a civil rights and political leader who is famous for making speeches to help African-Americans.

Jackie Robinson was the first African-American to play on a major-league baseball team and was inducted into the National Baseball Hall of Fame.

Mini-Book *(cont.)*

See page 67 for directions.

Mary McLeod Bethune worked to help educate African-Americans and worked with four presidents to further expand educational opportunities.

George Washington Carver was a scientist famous for agricultural research and for discovering the many uses of peanuts.

Harriet Tubman led hundreds of slaves to freedom in the North on the Underground Railroad.

Louis Armstrong was a famous jazz trumpet player and band leader.

Sojourner Truth was the first African-American woman to travel through the country making speeches against slavery.

Ralph Bunche worked at the United Nations and was the first African-American to win the Nobel Peace Prize.

Wilma Rudolph was the first African-American woman to win three gold medals for track at the Olympics.

Benjamin Banneker was an astronomer, mathematician, inventor, surveyor, and the first African-American to receive a presidential appointment.

Mini-Book *(cont.)*

See page 67 for directions.

Patricia Roberts Harris was the first African-American woman to serve as a United States Ambassador in another country.

Booker T. Washington was a teacher who founded the Tuskegee Institute to train African-Americans to become carpenters, farmers, mechanics, and teachers.

Shirley Chisholm was the first African-American woman to become a member of the United States Congress.

In 1983, Guion Bluford was the first African-American to go into space.

Marian Anderson became the first African-American soloist to sing with the Metropolitan Opera in New York City.

Phillis Wheatley had a book of poems published in 1773 and became the first major African-American poet.

Rosa Parks refused to give up her bus seat to a white passenger in Montgomery, Alabama. This helped to start the civil rights movement.

Matthew Henson, an African-American explorer, discovered the North Pole with Robert Peary.

Gung Hay Fat Choy

Author: June Behrens

Publisher: Childrens Press, 1982

Summary: Through expository text and colorful photographs, this book explains the importance of the Chinese New Year and how it is celebrated by Chinese-Americans.

Related Holiday: The Chinese New Year does not fall on the same date each year. It may come any time between the middle of January and the middle of February. The festival may be up to seven days in length.

Related Poetry: "Chinese New Year," Traditional Chinese Nursery Rhyme, *The Family Read-Aloud Holiday Treasury* (Little, Brown & Company, 1991)

Connecting Activities:

- Before your students enter the classroom on the Chinese New Year, use red bulletin board paper to make a good luck seal on the classroom door. Explain that Chinese custom says that whatever happens on the first day of the year may decide the events for the entire year.

- Explain to your students that the words "Gung Hay Fat Choy" mean Happy New Year in Chinese. Make a Gung Hay Fat Choy banner on red bulletin board paper. Use letters cut from gold foil wrapping paper. Try your hand at Chinese writing by painting the Chinese characters that correlate with the English words. Children may add details to the banner that show or tell about the celebration.

- Use the chart of the Chinese Lunar Calendar Horoscope on page 74 to have your students discover what the animal symbol was for the years in which they were born and the animal which represents the current year. Children may use watercolors to paint the animal for the year. Display these with the title "Year of the _____." People born within an animal's year are said to have the qualities of that animal. Ask students if they think they have those qualities.

- Make animal books that tell about the twelve animals of the Chinese Lunar Calendar. Include the characteristics of each animal.

- Have a Gung Hay Fat Choy snack. Since orange and red are regarded as the colors of joy, serve oranges and apples to your students to bring them good luck for the new year. Children may help in washing and preparing these fruits.

- Since the Chinese add a year to their age on New Year's Day, serve a birthday cake at your snack time, too. Make a "real graph" with your students to see if they would like to follow this custom, or if they would prefer to have their own birthdays. Have children line up in two lines to show their preferences.

72

Gung Hay Fat Choy (cont.)

- The climax of the celebration is the Golden Dragon Parade. Prepare copies of the dragon masks on page 75. These may be colored with paint, markers, or crayons and decorated with glitter and sequins. You might want to mount each mask on tag board to make it more sturdy. Have children cut out eye holes and staple the completed masks to a tongue depressor to make a mask suitable for wearing. The dragon is a sacred animal to the Chinese, the symbol of Chinese emperors, and a symbol of strength and goodness. Children could wear their dragon masks as they recite the poem mentioned in this unit.

- Have students make three-dimensional dragon heads beginning with a box large enough to fit over a child's head. Decorate the box with paint, paper scraps, tubes, egg cartons, curled tissue paper, crepe paper, and paper shapes. One child could wear this dragon head, while other children could have large brightly colored paper covering their heads as they follow along ''follow-the-leader'' style for your own classroom dragon parade. Children may take turns wearing their dragons' heads.

- Draw and decorate a dragon's head on a bulletin board. Attach construction paper sections for the dragon's body. Write one fact which the students learned about Chinese New Year onto each section of the dragon's body. Add the title ''Gung Hay Fat Choy'' to the display.

- Make envelopes from red construction paper. Reread the section in the book that explains ''Lai see,'' good luck money wrapped in red paper, which is given as a gift for the new year. Show your students a clear plastic container in which you have put many pennies. Have them estimate how many there are, and then work with them to count them into tens and ones to find the total amount. Use the pennies to put a penny or two (the same amount for each student) inside each of the red envelopes for each child as a souvenir of *Gung Hay Fat Choy*.

- If possible, invite a Chinese American into your classroom to tell about Chinese New Year and customs which make it such an important celebration in the Chinese culture.

- Make Chinese paper lanterns. Decorate a 9" x 12" (23 cm x 30 cm) piece of construction paper with Chinese characters. Fold it in half lengthwise and draw a line ½" (1.3 cm) from the edge. Cut even slits from the fold to the line. Open the paper, overlap uncut edges and staple them. Glue tissue paper pieces on the bottom edge. Add a paper handle on top, if desired.

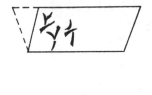

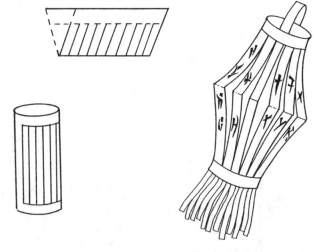

Chinese Horoscope

See page 72 for directions.

兎

Year of the Rabbit
1951, 1963, 1975, 1987, 1999, 2011
Characteristics: nice to be around; talkative; trustworthy

羊

Year of the Ram
1943, 1955, 1967, 1979, 1991, 2003
Characteristics: artistic; inquisitive; wise

猪

Year of the Boar
1947, 1959, 1971, 1983, 1995, 2007
Characteristics: good students; brave and honest; complete tasks

虎

Year of the Tiger
1950, 1962, 1974, 1986, 1998, 2010
Characteristics: brave; respected by others for their courage and deep thoughts

馬

Year of the Horse
1942, 1954, 1966, 1978, 1990, 2002
Characteristics: popular; spread cheer and compliments to others; hard workers

犬

Year of the Dog
1946, 1958, 1970, 1982, 1994, 2006
Characteristics: loyal; trustworthy; worry too much

牛

Year of the Ox
1949, 1961, 1973, 1985, 1997, 2009
Characteristics: dependable and calm; good listeners; have very definite ideas about things

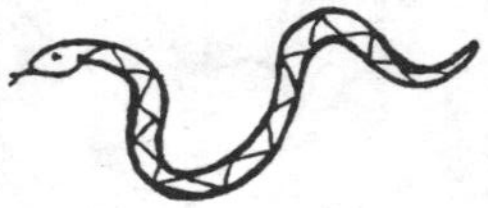

蛇

Year of the Snake
1941, 1953, 1965, 1977, 1989, 2001
Characteristics: loves books, food, plays, and music; known to have good fortune with money

雞

Year of the Rooster
1945, 1957, 1969, 1981, 1993, 2005
Characteristics: hard working; talented; think deep thoughts

鼠

Year of the Rat
1948, 1960, 1972, 1984, 1996, 2008
Characteristics: very popular people; good artists; inventors

龍

Year of the Dragon
1952, 1964, 1976, 1988, 2000, 2012
Characteristics: healthy and full of energy; good listeners

猴

Year of the Monkey
1944, 1956, 1968, 1980, 1992, 2004
Characteristics: humorous; good problem solvers

Paper Dragon Mask

Directions: Color or decorate the dragon mask. Cut out the eye holes and staple or glue the mask to a tongue depressor.

A Garden for a Groundhog

Author: Lorna Balian

Publisher: Humbug Press, 1985

Summary: As the O'Learys settle in for the winter on their small farm, the resident groundhog hibernates in his burrow beneath the apple tree. As Groundhog Day approaches, Mrs. O'Leary becomes concerned that the groundhog will devour their spring garden. Mr. O'Leary makes plans that are sure to please everyone. But somehow, even the best laid plans do not always unfold as they should!

Related Holiday: Groundhog Day is celebrated in North America on February 2nd. If the groundhog sees his shadow, he goes back in his burrow and that means six more weeks of winter. If his shadow is not seen, spring is on its way.

Related Poetry: "Groundhog, Groundhog," by Jean Warren, *Special Day Celebrations* (Warren Publishing House, 1989); "Ground Hog Day" by Lilian Moore, *The Random House Book of Poetry for Children* (Random House, 1983)

Connecting Activities:

- Discuss groundhogs and other animals that live underground. Make a list of animals that live in a burrow as groundhogs do. If possible, display non-fiction books and pictures which show the different section into which a burrow is divided, such as a sleeping area and a place to store food.

- Discuss what hibernation means. Talk about animals that hibernate during the winter as the groundhog in the story does. Mention that a groundhog is also called a woodchuck and is a member of the rodent family.

- Begin reading *A Garden for a Groundhog*. Compare the ways in which the O'Learys and the groundhog spent the winter. Ask children if they think the O'Learys were hibernating, too, and in what way. How were the O'Learys preparing for spring?

- When Mr. O'Leary tells the story of what the groundhog does on Groundhog Day, his wife calls it foolishness. Ask children for their opinions about the coming of spring based on the actions of a groundhog.

- With the exception of the groundhog, the animals and seasons do what they are supposed to do in the story. Talk about the various animals mentioned and describe their usual behaviors and habitats.

- While reading the story, stop at the section where Mr. O'Leary mentions a plan to keep the groundhog from eating most of the garden. Have children predict what his plan might be.

- After reading *A Garden for a Groundhog* do a story map, listing events from the beginning, middle, and end of the story. Ask students to write a new ending for the story.

A Garden for a Groundhog (cont.)

- Make a large mural of an underground area including such details as tree roots, rocks, and animal burrows and tunnels. Study the illustrations in the book for ideas or read *Under Your Feet* by Joanna Ryder (bibliography, page 93). Have each student make a small groundhog to place on the mural and name each groundhog. Think of a name for your groundhog habitat such as "Woodchuck Acres Estates." Label all the items found in the mural. This could also be done as a bulletin board.

- Each year, people gather in Pennsylvania to watch the groundhog emerge from its burrow. There actually is a groundhog club whose members attend this ceremony every February 2nd. Create a groundhog fan club in your classroom and write some membership rules. Design a special badge for club members to wear and write a special groundhog pledge (or say one of the groundhog poems listed at the beginning of this section).

- As part of the groundhog fan club activities, write a "Dear Mr. Groundhog" letter. Tell the groundhog why you do or do not want him to see his shadow. Ask him questions about himself, such as how he became groundhog for groundhog day.

- Make a chart listing "good things" and "bad things" about having six more weeks of winter. These ideas could be made into a class book. Or do a yes-no graph and have students vote on whether they would like six more week of winter. This can be done easily by drawing a line down the center of a large piece of tag board, and labeling one side "yes" and the other side "no." At the top of the graph write the question "Do you want six more weeks of winter?" Each student can vote by clipping a clothespin labeled with his or her name on the appropriate side of the graph.

- After finding out the groundhog's prediction for this year, count out six weeks on a calendar. Each day, record the weather in order to check if the weather did stay wintery or become mild. If you live in an area of the country where the weather stays mild, chart the weather in a more variable part of the country. You can do this easily by looking at a national weather map in the newspaper.

- For a related science activity, discuss light and shadows. Talk about sources of light (sun, lamp, etc.) and how shadows are made. On a sunny day, go outside and look for shadows. Using chalk, let students outline each other's shadows. Compare shadows at different times of the day (morning, noon, and afternoon).

- Make groundhog puppets. Give each child a brown paper lunch bag, scissors, glue, markers or crayons, and a copy of the pattern pieces on page 78. Glue the head on the folded sack's bottom, as shown. Make an outline of the body on the bag, starting underneath the bottom flap where the head was glued. Add the hands, feet, and tail. To use, put arm in bag and move head flap. Recite some of the groundhog poems or sing the songs found at the beginning of the section. Students may write or copy a favorite poem to paste on the back of the bag.

Groundhog Puppet

See page 77 for directions.

Four Valentines in a Rainstorm

Author: Felicia Bond

Publisher: Thomas Y. Crowell, 1983

Summary: A valentine rainstorm provides Cornelia Augusta with many hearts which she uses to make valentines for all of her friends. This clever book provides many opportunities for students to predict as they read.

Related Holiday: Valentine's Day is a day to recognize the people you love. It is celebrated on February 14th in the United States, Canada, and Europe.

Related Poetry: ''My Valentine'' by Myra Cohn Livingston, *Celebrations* (Warren Publishing House, 1988); *It's Valentine's Day* by Jack Prelutsky (Scholastic, 1985)

Related Songs: ''Special Friend'' and ''I Get Valentines'' by Patricia Coyne, *Holiday Piggyback Songs* (Warren Publishing House, 1988)

Connecting Activities:

- To create interest before reading the story, give a red paper heart to each student. Emphasize creative thinking by having the children invent new uses for the heart. For example, a heart shape could be a butterfly's wing or a vase for flowers. Encourage the children to try turning the heart different ways and even folding it for new ideas. List of all of the ideas that the class brainstorms.

- Discuss the unusual title and what it might mean. As the story is being read, ask the children to listen and try to add the number of valentines mentioned. This activity promotes careful listening, problem solving skills, and mental math.

- Divide the class into small cooperative groups of four to five students. Give each group the same hearts that Cornelia found during the rainstorm. The students try to create as many new valentines as they can. Have each student designate a valentine for someone specific. It could be for an animal (as the girl did in the story), a person, or even an imaginary character such as Mickey Mouse. The design of the heart should reflect some quality of the character to whom it is being given.

- Valentine's Day provides a good opportunity to recognize school personnel and let them know how much they're appreciated all year long. The school secretary, paraprofessionals, custodians, and lunchroom and recess supervisors would all enjoy receiving a card signed by the whole class. Sing a valentine's song as you deliver the cards.

- Take a trip to the post office to find out how valentines get to our mailboxes. Invite a mail carrier to come to the classroom to explain how the process works. Read *The Post Office Book: Mail and How It Moves* by Gail Gibbons (see bibliography, page 93). This book describes the history of the postal service as well as the operation of the modern day post office. Have a stamp collector introduce the class to stamp collecting.

Four Valentines in a Rainstorm *(cont.)*

- Try some of these art activities for a "Hearty Art" bulletin board. First, fold an 18" (46 cm) square piece of red or white butcher paper in half. Draw a heart shape and cut out the hearts. Paint an identical pattern or design on both hearts. When dry, place the hearts together (design side facing out), stuff with newspaper and staple to make a heart "pillow."

- Use some old magazines and cards for a collage of hearts. Cut many different sizes of hearts out of magazine pictures. Try to find pictures that have a lot of red in them or are brightly colored. Glue the hearts in a pleasing arrangement on a 9" x 12" (23 cm x 30 cm) piece of white construction paper. Decorate between the hearts by drawing with crayon or marker or use pictures from old cards to add to your collage.

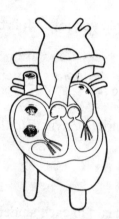

- Discuss how the real heart functions and look at a diagram of a heart. During gym class, have the students check their resting pulses and then check pulses again after exercise. Talk about the importance of a warm-up and a cool-down period before and after physical activity. This would be a great opportunity to have a doctor or a nutritionist visit as a guest speaker. Their emphasis could be on ways to be "heart smart." Include healthy practices and the importance of nutrition and exercise.

- In the math center, fill a jar with candy conversation hearts. Estimate how many hearts are in the jar. The hearts can also be grouped by tens and counted, or used for some hands-on adding and subtracting. Tell the students a story problem and have them act it out with the hearts. Have students create their own problems.

- Ask the students to bring in a variety of candy boxes. Use the boxes in a special "Sweet Treats" math center. Sort and classify the boxes by different categories such as size, shape and color. Compare and weigh them on a balance scale. Or, have students count out the correct amount of play money to "buy" a box of candy.

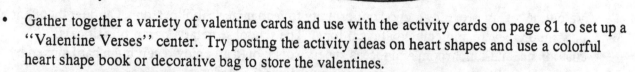

- Gather together a variety of valentine cards and use with the activity cards on page 81 to set up a "Valentine Verses" center. Try posting the activity ideas on heart shapes and use a colorful heart shape book or decorative bag to store the valentines.

- Finally, to learn more about the history of Valentine's Day, an excellent reference book is *Hearts, Cupids, and Red Roses* by Edna Barth (see bibliography, page 93). This book explores the meaning of the various symbols of the holiday, such as heart shapes, cupids, and lace.

Valentine Verses Cards

See page 80 for directions.

 Count all of the cards. Group by tens as you count.

 Arrange ten cards in order from smallest to largest.

 Count how many times the word "love" appears on ten of the valentines.

 Sort the cards using your own categories.

 Choose 5 valentines. Add the prices to determine how much you would have to pay.

 Arrange 10 cards in order from least expensive to most expensive.

 Choose 5 cards. Survey your classmates to find out which card is the favorite.

 Write down 10 words from one of the cards. Arrange the words in alphabetical order.

 Choose your favorite card. Write a new verse for the inside.

 Make a list of the people to whom you will send valentines (Mom, Dad, friend, etc.).

George Washington's Breakfast

Author: Jean Fritz

Publisher: Trumpet Club, 1969

Summary: This story tells of a modern-day boy, George Washington Allen, who learns many facts about George Washington as he searches to find out the answer to the question "What did George Washington eat for breakfast?"

Just Like Abraham Lincoln

Author: Bernard Waber

Publisher: Houghton Mifflin, 1964

Summary: This book tells the story of a young boy and his neighbor, Mr. Potts, who looks just like Abraham Lincoln and knows many facts about Mr. Lincoln.

Related Holiday: President's Day is celebrated in the United States on the third Monday in February to honor George Washington, the first President of the United States, whose birthday was on February 22, 1732, and Abraham Lincoln, the sixteenth President of the United States, whose birthday was on February 12, 1809.

Related Poetry: *My First President's Day Book* by Aileen Fisher (Childrens Press, 1987); "President's Day" by Myra Cohn Livingston, *Celebrations* (Holiday House, 1985); "Abraham Lincoln" by Rosemary Carr and Stephen Vincent Benet, *The Family Read-Aloud Holiday Treasury* (Little, Brown & Company, 1991); "Lincoln" and "Washington" by Nancy Byrd Turner, *The Random House Book of Poetry for Children* (Random House, 1983)

Related Songs: "Abraham Lincoln" and "George Washington" by Vicki Claybrook, *Holiday Piggyback Songs* (Warren Publishing House, 1988)

Connecting Activities:

- To correlate with *Just Like Abraham Lincoln*, try the following activities.

    — Have your students predict as you are reading what the boy's idea is when he whispers to his teacher. Predict again where Mr. Potts is going on February 12th in his frock coat.

George Washington's Breakfast; Just Like Abraham Lincoln (cont.)

— Make a comparison chart to compare and contrast Mr. Potts and Abraham Lincoln. Show how they are alike and how they are different, including appearance, when they lived, occupation, clothing, height, favorite things to do, etc.

— Read a copy of the Gettysburg Address to your students and discuss why it is such a famous speech. Explain how long ago "four score and seven years" was. (A score is equal to twenty years.)

— Encourage your students to extend the story and write their own stories to include the boy's new neighbor, Mr. Pettigrew, who happens to look just like George Washington.

• To correlate with *George Washington's Breakfast*, try the following activities.

— Share that the purpose for listening to the book is to find out what George Washington had for breakfast.

— Have your students predict what George Washington might have had for breakfast and list their ideas on chart paper. After you've read the book, see how accurate their predictions were.

— List the methods which George (the boy) utilized in his detective work to find out more information (library, interviewing, books, visiting a museum, etc.) about George Washington.

— Discuss the Smithsonian Institution and Mount Vernon as real places that the public can visit. Refer your students to *The Inside-Outside Book of Washington, D.C.* by Roxie Munro or *A Visit to Washington, D.C.* by Jill Krementz (see bibliography, page 93).

— Since George Washington and George Washington Allen both liked to count buttons and steps, set up a counting center at your math area. Have your students count the total number of buttons that are being worn in your classroom on a given day. Count the number of steps you take as you walk from your classroom to the school office or out onto the playground.

— Make hoecakes or cornbread with your students.

— Encourage your students to extend the book by predicting and then finding out what George Washington Allen's next research project was going to be (finding out what George Washington ate for lunch).

• Try the following activities after you have read both books:

— Compare pictures of the United States flag as it looked during Washington's time, Lincoln's time, and the present.

George Washington's Breakfast;
Just Like Abraham Lincoln (cont.)

— Enlarge the hats on pages 85 and 86. Summarize facts about each of the presidents on the appropriate hats. Laminate your hats and use a water soluble marker, so that you can wash the hats off and reuse them next year. Use the hat shapes to make covers for class books about each president. Have each child do one page for each president, beginning with a sentence starter such as "My favorite fact about George Washington (Abraham Lincoln) is that he _____." Make a story roll-up about each president. Children work in cooperative groups to illustrate the main events in each man's life on a long piece of bulletin board paper in the correct sequential order. Roll up the story and unroll it as you tell about the president's life.

• Discuss the lives of Americans at the time of Washington and at the time of Lincoln. Refer to *If You Grew Up with George Washington* by Ruth Belov Gross and *If You Grew Up with Abraham Lincoln* by Ann McGovern (see bibliography, page 93).

• Discuss currency and coins which have pictures of these presidents.

• Try some presidential graphing. Have your students "vote" as they enter the classroom to answer the question "Who do you like best, Washington or Lincoln?" Have two clear tennis ball cans decorated with U.S. flag stickers and a slit cut in the top of each. One can is labeled George Washington and the other is labeled Abraham Lincoln. To register their votes, children place a real or play quarter into the Washington can or a real or play penny into the Lincoln can (to correlate with their pictures on the coins). Take the money out of the cans to make a real graph on the floor. Tally the coins and count by ones to find out the total money for Lincoln and count by twenty-fives to find out the total money for Washington. Children may work in small groups to investigate the coins (list all of the things and words found on the coins, make rubbings of the coins, etc). Have children transfer their preferences to a picture graph using coin stamps to record their choices.

Who do you like best?

George	O	O	O	O	O	
Abe	O	O	O	O	O	O

• Provide a "Coin Count of the Day" for your students. Purchase or make large, laminated coin shapes to use in this activity. Put out an age-appropriate amount of coins on the board or at a money center. Children record the amount which they believe the coins represent on a small piece of paper and place the paper in a toy bank. At the end of the school day, count the coin values together and see how many students were correct on their independent coin counting.

• Use a calculator to find out how old George Washington and Abraham Lincoln would be if they were alive today. Also, use the calculator to determine how long ago the Gettysburg Address was written. Find out how many years have passed since the occurrence of other historical facts relating to Washington and Lincoln.

Abraham Lincoln's Stovepipe Hat

See page 84 for directions.

George Washington's Three Cornered Hat

See page 84 for directions.

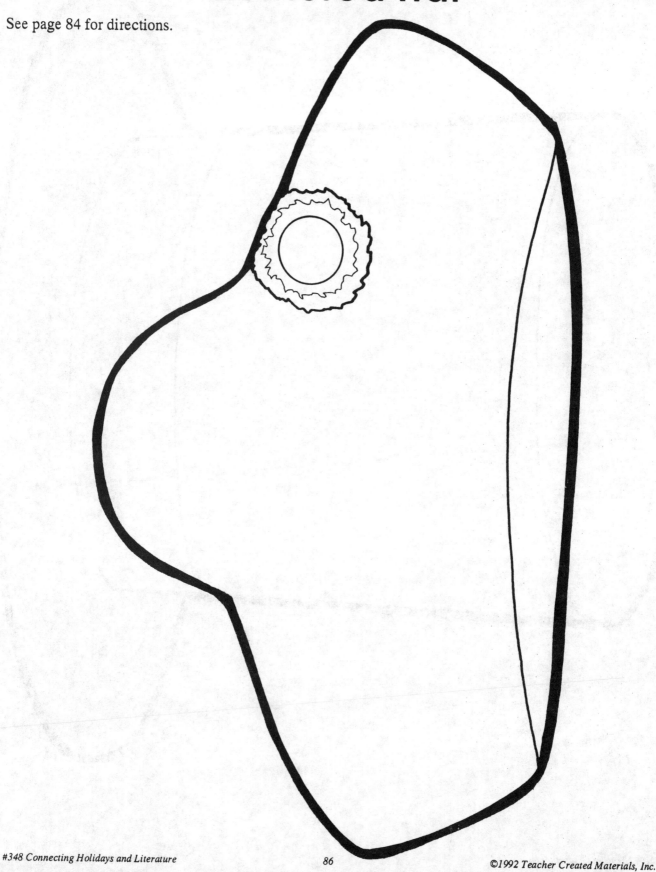

St. Patrick's Day in the Morning

Author: Eve Bunting

Publisher: Clarion Books, 1980

Summary: A young Irish boy named Jamie gets up early on St. Patrick's Day to celebrate the holiday with his own parade. The charming illustrations show scenes from a small village in Ireland.

Related Holiday: St. Patrick's Day is an Irish holiday celebrated on March 17th in honor of St. Patrick, the patron saint of Ireland.

Related Poetry: "Saint Patrick's Day" by Myra Cohn Livingston, *Celebrations* (Scholastic, 1985)

Related Songs: "Catch Him If You Can" by Maureen Gutyan, *Holiday Piggyback Songs* (Warren Publishing House, 1988)

Connecting Activities:

- Give each child a paper shamrock to wear while listening to the story. Discuss the Irish custom for St. Patrick's Day called "the wearing of the green." This ancient custom originated as an important symbol of springtime and of hope. Talk about how shamrocks also symbolize good luck. Brainstorm a list of other items which symbolize good luck such as a horseshoe or a rabbit's foot.

- Discuss the country of Ireland and the history of St. Patrick. Two very good sources are *Patrick, Patron Saint of Ireland* by Tomie dePaola and *Shamrocks, Harps, and Shillelaghs, The Story of the St. Patrick's Day Symbols* by Edna Barth. Both books contain a wealth of information on the origins of St. Patrick's Day.

- Talk about the Irish lore of the mischievous leprechaun. Find a leprechaun doll in a toy store or card shop (many stores carry such items for St. Patrick's Day). Have your class name the leprechaun and keep him in the room as your lucky mascot during March. It's especially fun if the leprechaun plays harmless pranks during the night, such as hiding the reading books or mixing up the childrens' shoes (with a little help from the teacher, of course!).

- In your math center, put out a jar filled with pennies or candy coins to resemble gold coins. Estimate how many coins are in the "pot of gold." Place the pot at the end of a large laminated rainbow. If you laminate the rainbow, the estimates can be written on the rainbow using a wipe-off pen. Group the pennies or candy coins by tens, and count to check your estimates.

- Enjoy a treasure hunt using the "pot of gold" coins. Hide one hundred coins in the classroom (or any amount that you wish) and let the students work in teams to find as many coins as they can. Try timing the treasure hunt. Group the coins by tens and total them. Estimate the total weight of the coins and check the weight on a balance scale.

St. Patrick's Day in the Morning *(cont.)*

- Make potato prints. Prepare the potatoes by carving a design into half of a raw potato. The excess potato has to be cut away leaving a raised design. The potato is then dipped into tempera paint, and pressed on a piece of construction paper to make a potato print picture. Try using bright green paint on yellow construction paper for a nice effect.

- Make some lucky headbands to wear on St. Patrick's Day. Cut 2" (5 cm) strips of white or yellow construction paper long enough to go around a child's head and staple it to make headbands. Then have each student cut out three green shamrocks. On each shamrock, the students write a wish and the shamrocks are glued onto the headband. A hot glue gun may be used to add pennies to the headband if desired.

- Wrap up your celebration by bringing in green cupcakes and green milk for a treat. Pistachio pudding also works well. Play some traditional Irish music (usually available at the public library) and try to dance an Irish jig.

- Rainbows are often associated with the leprechaun's pot of gold. For some activities involving rainbows see *Connecting Science and Literature* (TCM341).

- Use the research cards provided on page 89 to create a "Lucky Learning" center in your room. Cut out each card. Glue it to an index card and laminate. Or, reproduce the page directly onto index paper before cutting. Include some of the books mentioned in previous activities. Students locate the answers to the questions in the books.

- Reproduce the cards on page 92 and game board on pages 90-91 to play the "Lucky Coins" game. Color, mount on tag board, and laminate the game board and cards. Or, reproduce the pages on index paper. Players take turns drawing a card. They must correctly identify the amount represented on the card. If desired, provide each group of players with a set of real coins (nickel, penny, quarter, dime) to use in identifying and adding the card coins. The player then counts how many coins are on the card and moves that number of spaces. For example, if the card has two coins, you move two spaces. Add an answer key to the back of the game for the coin cards (letter A = 15 cents).

- Celebrate St. Patrick's Day with a variety of art projects. Using tempera paint, have the students paint portraits of leprechauns. Under each painting, put a sentence strip with an alliterative statement describing the leprechauns. One example would be "Lucky leprechauns leap lightly on logs."

Lucky Learning Cards

See page 88 for directions.

 Why is Ireland called the Emerald Isle?

 Where was St. Patrick born?

 What job did St. Patrick have when he first came to Ireland?

 Why are there no snakes in Ireland?

 What is "the wearin' of the green?"

 What are the colors on the Irish flag?

 Why is the shamrock used as a symbol of St. Patrick's Day?

 What is a Shillelagh?

 What is a leprechaun and what does he do?

 Why is the potato important in Ireland?

Lucky Coins

See directions on page 88.

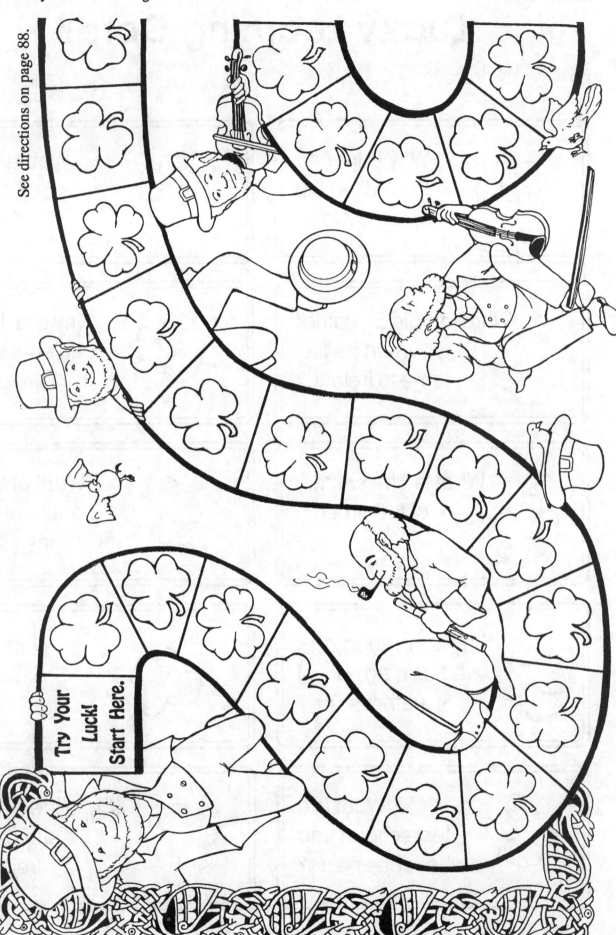

Try Your
Luck!
Start Here.

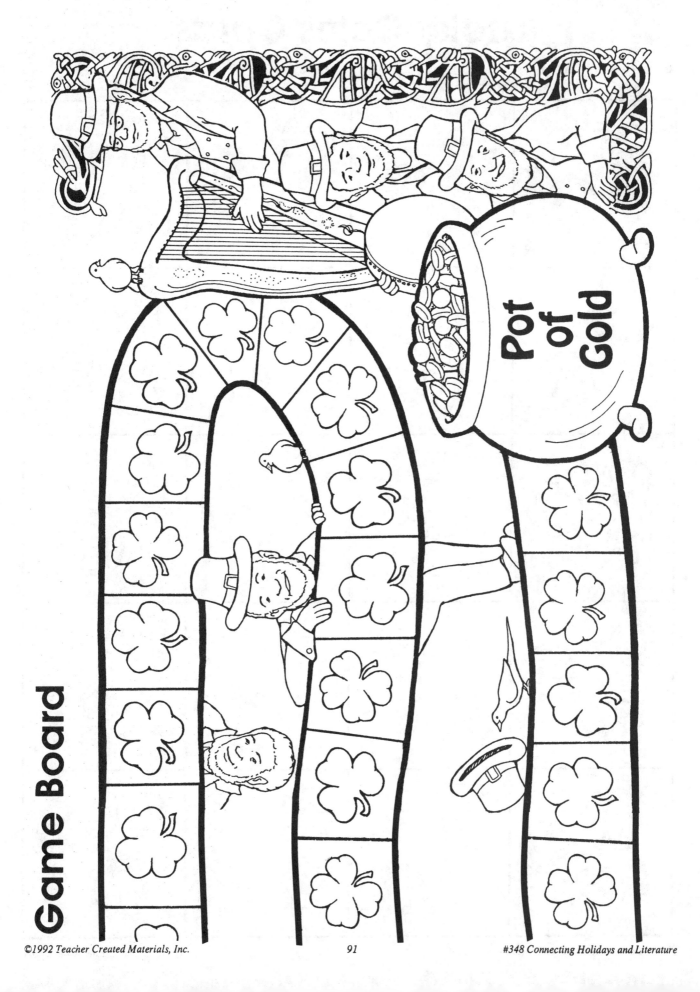

Game Board

Pot of Gold

Lucky Coins Cards

See page 88 for directions.

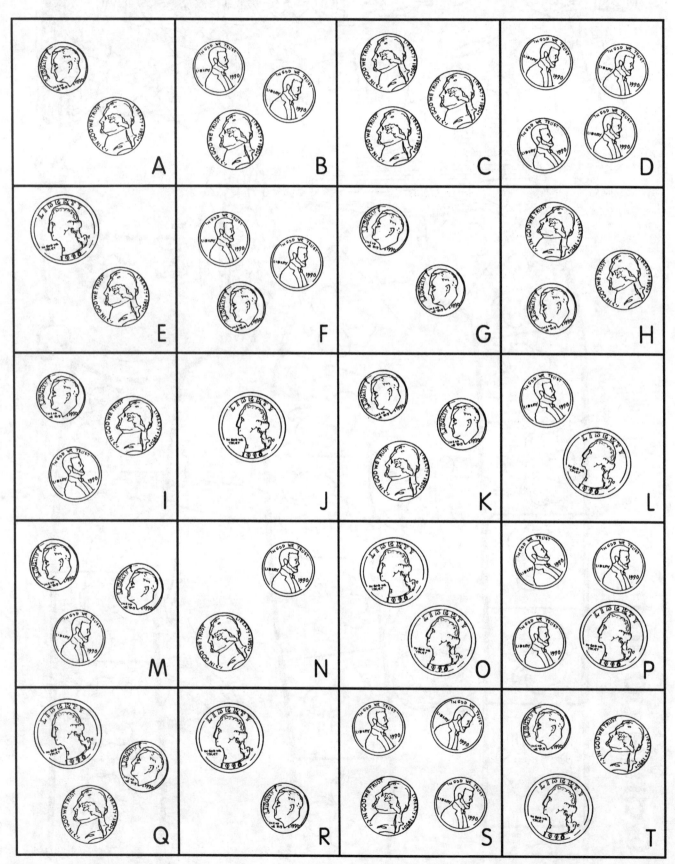

Wonderful Winter Bibliography

Adler, David A. *A Picture Book of Hanukkah* (Holiday House, 1982)

Adler, David A. *A Picture Book of Martin Luther King, Jr.* (Holiday House, 1989)

Ahlberg, Janet & Allan. *The Jolly Christmas Postman* (Little, Brown & Company, 1991)

Barry, Robert. *Mr. Willowby's Christmas Tree* (McGraw-Hill, 1963)

Barth, Edna. *Hearts, Cupids, and Red Roses: The Story of Valentine Symbols* (Clarion Books, 1974)

Barth, Edna. *Holly, Reindeer, and Colored Lights: The Story of the Christmas Symbols* (Clarion Books, 1971)

Bemelmans, Ludwig. *Madeline's Christmas* (Viking Penguin, 1985)

Berenstain, Stan & Jan. *The Berenstain Bears' Christmas Tree* (Random House, 1980)

Brett, Jan. *The Wild Christmas Reindeer* (G.P. Putnam's Sons, 1990)

Bridwell, Norman. *Clifford's Christmas* (Scholastic, 1984)

Brown, Marc. *Arthur's Christmas* (Little, Brown & Company, 1984)

Brown, Marc. *Arthur's Valentine* (Little, Brown & Company, 1980)

Bunting, Eve. *The Valentine Bears* (Clarion Books, 1983)

Burden-Patmon, Denise. *Imani's Gift at Kwanzaa* (Modern Curriculum Press, 1992)

Carlson, Nancy. *Take Time to Relax!* (Viking, 1991)

Cheng, Hou-tien. *The Chinese New Year* (Holt, Rinehart & Winston, 1976)

Chiemroum, Sothea. *Dara's Cambodian New Year* (Modern Curriculum Press, 1992)

Chocolate, Deborah M. Newton. *Kwanzaa* (Childrens Press, 1990)

dePaola, Tomie. *My First Chanukah* (G.P. Putnam's Sons, 1989)

Ets, Marie Hall & Aurora Labastida. *Nine Days to Christmas: A Story of Mexico* (Viking Press, 1959)

Gibbons, Gail. *Christmas Time* (Holiday House, 1982)

Gibbons, Gail. *Valentine's Day* (Holiday House, 1986)

Gibbons, Gail. *The Post Office Book: Mail & How It Moves* (Harper Jr., 1986)

Goldin, Barbara Diamond. *The World's Birthday: A Rosh Hashanah Story* (HBJ, 1990)

Groner, Judye & Madeline Wikler. *All About Hanukkah* (Kar-Ben Copies, 1988)

Gross, Ruth Belov. *If You Grew Up With George Washington* (Scholastic, 1982)

Henderson, Kathy. *Christmas Trees* (Childrens Press, 1989)

Houston, Gloria. *The Year of the Perfect Christmas Tree* (Dial Books, 1988)

Johnson, Crockett. *Will Spring Be Early? or Will Spring Be Late?* (Harper & Row, 1959)

Kelley, Emily. *Christmas Around the World* (Carolrhoda Books, 1986)

Krementz, Jill. *A Visit to Washington D.C.* (Scholastic, 1987)

Low, Alice. *The Family Read-Aloud Christmas Treasury* (Joy Street/Little, Brown & Company, 1989)

Lowery, Linda. *Martin Luther King Day* (Scholastic, 1987)

Luenn, Nancy. *Nessa's Fish* (Atheneum, 1990)

Manushkin, Fran. *Latkes and Applesauce* (Scholastic, 1990)

McGovern, Ann. *If You Grew Up With Abraham Lincoln* (Scholastic, 1992)

Modell, Frank. *Goodbye Old Year, Hello New Year* (Greenwillow Books, 1984)

Munro, Roxie. *The Inside-Outside Book of Washington, D.C.* (Dutton, 1987)

Polacco, Patricia. *Uncle Vova's Tree* (Philomel Books, 1989)

Prelutsky, Jack. *It's Valentine's Day* (Greenwillow Books, 1983)

Ryder, Joanne. *White Bear, Ice Bear* (Morrow Junior Books, 1989)

Schweninger, Ann. *Valentine Friends* (Puffin Books, 1988)

Sing, Rachel. *Chinese New Year's Dragon* (Modern Curriculum Press, 1992)

Spier, Peter. *Peter Spier's Christmas!* (Doubleday, 1983)

Tran, Kim-Lan. *Tet: The New Year* (Modern Curriculum Press, 1992)

Wallace, Ian. *Chin Chiang and the Dragon's Dance* (Atheneum, 1984)

Waters, Kate & Madeline Slovenz-Low. *Lion Dancer: Ernie Wan's Chinese New Year* (Scholastic, 1990)

Rechenka's Eggs

Author: Patricia Polacco

Publisher: Philomel Books, 1988

Summary: This delightful tale tells of Babushka, a champion painter of colorful eggs for the Easter Festival in Moskva, who rescues an injured goose, that in turn lays fourteen very special eggs before it returns to its flock.

Related Holiday: Easter is a Christian holiday, which falls in March or April, to celebrate the Resurrection of Jesus.

Related Poetry: "Easter: For Penny" by Myra Cohn Livingston, *Celebrations* (Holiday House, 1985); "Baby Chick" by Aileen Fisher, "Animals Animals" (Philomel Books, 1989); "The Sun on Easter Day" by Norma Farber, *The Family Read-Aloud Holiday Treasury* (Little, Brown & Company, 1991)

Related Songs: "Easter Eggs" by Maureen Gutyan, "Easter, Easter" by Colraine Pettipaw Hunley, and "I'm a Little Chicken" by Susan Peters, *Holiday Piggyback Songs* (Warren Publishing House, 1988)

Connecting Activities:

- Have a basket of decorated eggs in your story area to motivate your students as you read *Rechenka's Eggs*. Before you read the book, explain to your students that the author, Patricia Polacco, enjoys painting Ukrainian eggs like those on the cover and inside the book, since her family came from the Ukraine and Georgian provinces in Russia. The Ukrainian folk art of decorating eggs is called Pysanky (pi SAN kee). Show your students where this area is on a globe or world map, and explain that the Soviet Union's republics are now separate countries.

- Make a story map to show the main events of the story on egg shapes. Work with your students to list the eight main events in the story on the chalkboard. Write one event on each egg. Children may work in groups to illustrate each event. Display these on a bulletin board, adding the title of the story, too.

- Point out to your students the many Russian items or words which are included in the book: Old Moskva (Moscow) with its onion domes, dacha, kulich, pashka, and neit. Ask students if they can derive the meanings for these words from the context. Read a factual book about this area to your class to find out more about the history of this area. One such source is *The Soviet Union* by Karen Jacobsen (see bibliography, page 118), which contains photographs of the onion domes in Moscow. Watch for newspaper articles about the changes happening now in these countries, such as their new flags and new governments.

- Try some Russian foods with your students. The book *Cooking the Russian Way* by Gregory and Rita Plotkin (see bibliography, page 118) contains several easy and authentic recipes.

Rechenka's Eggs (cont.)

- Encourage your students to predict if the baby gosling will lay decorated eggs or plain eggs. Children could extend this idea to create their own original endings for the story.

- You might try making eggs similar to the way Babushka did in the book. First, make small holes at both ends of the eggs. Then blow the yolk and white into a dish. Rinse the eggs with warm water and carefully pat them dry. Gently use markers to decorate the eggs. (You could ask parents to send in eggshells that have already been blown out and packaged carefully in egg cartons or ask for parent volunteers to do the work at school.)

- Color the eggs on page 96 with bright markers, making sure that each egg is exactly like its match. Mount the page on tag board, cut out the eggs, and laminate them. Place the eggs in a clear, resealable plastic bag and then put the bag of eggs in a basket of Easter grass in your story area. Have students pair up to play "Egg Concentration" in which they find matching pairs of eggs. To play, put the eggs face down on a table. Turn over two cards, one at a time, to find identical eggs. If a match is made, the player keeps the pair. If not, the player turns the eggs face down and the next player takes a turn.

- For science, have students work in pairs to do some of the following egg experiments:

  — Give each pair of students a hard-boiled egg and a raw egg. Demonstrate how to try spinning the eggs on the floor, explaining that the one that is hard-boiled will spin. Have students determine which one of their eggs is hard-boiled and which is raw.

  — Put a dot of red food coloring on the shell of the hard-boiled egg. Leave it alone for an hour. Pull the eggshell off. The children should notice that the egg has a red dot, which shows that the eggshell has tiny holes that allow air and moisture to get inside for a developing chick. Examine the eggshell with a magnifying glass to see the tiny holes.

  — Use a bent paper clip to simulate a chick's beak. Peck with the paper clip on a raw egg to see how difficult it is for a baby chick to break through the egg's shell.

- Read a variety of books about eggs and animals that hatch from eggs, such as *Chickens Aren't the Only Ones* by Ruth Heller and *Egg to Chick* by Millicent E. Selsam (see bibliography, page 118). Set up an incubator with fertilized eggs in your classroom. Observe the hatching process first-hand. (See TCM256 *Thematic Unit — Birds*, for directions on making an incubator.)

Egg Concentration Game

See page 95 for directions.

The Tale of Peter Rabbit

Author: Beatrix Potter

Publisher: Penguin, 1902, 1989

Summary: Follow Peter Rabbit through Mr. McGregor's garden in this classic tale. Children will enjoy the beautiful illustrations and the delightful characters, Peter, Flopsy, Mopsy, and Cotton-tail.

Related Holiday: Easter is a very important holiday for Christians and is celebrated on a Sunday in March or April. Easter is considered to be a celebration of spring and of rebirth.

Related Poetry: "Easter: For Penny" by Myra Cohn Livingston, *Celebrations* (Scholastic, 1985): "Hunting Eggs" by Annetta E. Dellinger, *My First Easter Book* (Childrens Press, 1985)

Related Songs: "Here Comes Peter Cottontail" by Steve Nelson and Jack Rollins (Chappell & Company, 1950)

Connecting Activities:

- Assess the students' prior knowledge by doing a word web with the word "rabbit." Have them think of as many words as they can that relate to that word. As you do the web, talk about the characteristics of rabbits. Bring in some informational books about the many breeds of rabbits and talk about differences in color, size, habitat, and habits.

- Before reading the story, ask the students if they have ever heard of Beatrix Potter. Hold up *The Tale of Peter Rabbit* and some of her other books. Talk about the characters and their unusual names and how the animals talk and act like people. Put out an Easter basket and fill it with some Beatrix Potter books for use in the reading center.

- After reading the story, discuss what lesson Peter might have learned from his encounter with Mr. McGregor. Ask the students what parts of the story reflect the behaviors of real rabbits, and which parts are fantasy. Discuss vocabulary words that might be unfamiliar such as camomile tea.

- Beatrix Potter's inspiration for her books came from observing animals on her farm. Go outside the school to sit quietly and observe birds, squirrels, and whatever animals you might have in your area. Or, take a nature walk in a forest or nature center as a field trip. Students can sketch the animals that they have seen, just as the author did for her books. Add watercolor paints to complete the pictures.

- Make a list of all the Beatrix Potter books, the characters, and what type of animals they are. Put a star by any animals that live in your neighborhood or backyard. Make a mural showing your neighborhood and the animals that live there.

The Tale of Peter Rabbit *(cont.)*

- After your nature observations, have each student choose a favorite animal that he or she has seen. Or, bring in some photographs from children's nature magazines such as *Our Big Backyard* and *Ranger Rick* (appendix, page 144, National Wildlife Federation) and have them select one that they like. The students can name their animals as Beatrix Potter might have done, and write adventures for their new characters.

- Bring some nature into your classroom by having a class pet such as a rabbit or a hamster. If you don't want to have a permanent guest, students may take turns bringing in their caged pets for a visit of two or three days. Let each student sit quietly and observe the pet for five minutes. While they are watching, they can record everything they see and hear in a science journal. Some of the information could be compiled and illustrated to make a class book about your visitors.

- This story has a nice sequence of events which could be displayed as a story map. Cut about five large carrot shapes using orange and green construction paper and record the important events of the story. Mix the carrots up and have the students put the events back in sequence. Reproduce the stick puppets on page 99, and have them move from carrot to carrot as the story is retold.

- Peter Rabbit is well known for his little blue jacket. Have the students draw or paint Peter Rabbit in a brand new outfit, specifically designed for Easter. Create some new outfits for Flopsy, Mopsy, and Cotton-tail, too!

- Beatrix Potter is a very interesting author to learn about. Some good references on her life include *Nothing Is Impossible — the Story of Beatrix Potter* by Dorothy Aldis and *The Country Artist: A Story about Beatrix Potter* by David R. Collins (see bibliography, page 118). Make a mini-book to take home containing facts about Beatrix Potter's life (page 100).

- Brainstorm a list of vegetables and mark the ones that rabbits might eat. Talk about which vegetables grow in your area and then bring in some unusual vegetables for the children to sample. Do a yes-no graph to tell which vegetables students liked and disliked. A good picture book containing names of many vegetables is *Eating the Alphabet, Fruits and Vegetables from A to Z* by Lois Ehlert (see bibliography, page 118).

Do you like . . .?	yes	no
squash		
turnips		
zucchini		
rhubarb		

- In gym class, practice hopping like a rabbit. Try hopping on one foot, then the other. Have a hopping race or relay. Finally, try to learn the classic bunny hop dance. Besides being fun, the dance reinforces the basic concepts of right, left, forward, and back.

Stick Puppets

Directions: Color, cut out, and glue the stick puppets to wooden craft sticks. Use them to retell the story of Peter Rabbit.

Mini-Book

Color the pictures. Cut out the mini-book pages along the dashed lines. Arrange the book in the correct page order and staple.

Beatrix Potter
Mini-Book

This book belongs to

_____

1. Beatrix Potter was born in London, England in 1866.

2. She liked to draw and paint.

3. She lived on a farm and liked to watch little animals.

4. The story of *The Tale of Peter Rabbit* started out as a letter sent to a sick friend.

5. Beatrix Potter's favorite book was *The Tailor of Gloucester*, which is about some mice.

6. Some of her other books are *The Tale of Squirrel Nutkin* and *The Tale of Jeremy Fisher*.

7. Beatrix Potter's delightful animal characters are very popular to this day.

Arthur's April Fool

Author: Marc Brown

Publisher: Little, Brown & Company, 1983

Summary: This book tells of the lovable Arthur and his friends as they prepare for April Fool's Day and learn to deal with a bully named Binky Barnes.

Related Holiday: April Fool's Day, celebrated on April 1st, has its origins in France. Originally celebrated as the New Year, this was a time for gift giving, but when the new calendar was adopted near the end of the sixteenth century, some continued celebrating and were called ''April Fools.'' Now it is traditionally a day for practical jokes.

Related Poetry: ''April Fool'' by Myra Cohn Livingston, *Celebrations* (Holiday House, 1985)

Related Songs: ''April Fool's Day'' and ''All Around the Town Today'' by Jean Warren, *Holiday Piggyback Songs* (Warren Publishing House, 1988)

Connecting Activities:

- For a festive touch, wear a black top hat when you read this book to your class, since the characters are getting ready for a magic show in the book.

- As you are reading, pause at the point where Binky Barnes begins bothering Arthur. Divide your students into cooperative groups to do some problem solving. Give each group the task of coming up with a workable answer to this question: How could Arthur handle Binky and convince Binky to stop bothering him? Give each group five minutes to reach a solution, and then have each group report their solution to the class. Finish reading the book to see how the author, Marc Brown, has Arthur handle the problem.

- Your students may make a story map of the main events of *Arthur's April Fool* on black top hats, using the hat pattern on page 85 for this independent follow-up reading activity.

- On a chart, make a list of all of the April Fool's tricks found in the book. Encourage your students to study the illustrations carefully, as many are shown in illustrations but not mentioned in the text. Begin your list with tricks such as soap and toothpaste cookies, sneezing powder, and mixed nuts cans with snakes inside.

- Students would enjoy learning to print ''Happy April Fool's Day'' in a mirror image, as Arthur does in the book. Practice this on scrap paper first, checking its accuracy in a mirror. Then have each of your students make a Happy April Fool's Day badge to wear for your celebration. The words on the badge should appear in such a way that they can be seen correctly only in a mirror.

Arthur's April Fool (cont.)

- Discuss the difference between harmless pranks that are fun for everyone and pranks that could be dangerous or hurt other's feelings. In *Arthur's April Fool* the pranks were harmless, and any pranks which your students consider playing on others should also be harmless. Make a list of possible and appropriate April Fool's Day tricks which they could play on their families.

- Read some factual books on April Fool's Day and its origin to your class (or have them available for your students to read independently), such as *April Fool* by Mary Blount Christian and *April Fool's Day* by Dorothy LesTina (see bibliography, page 118).

- Have a class magic show on April Fool's Day. Demonstrate a few simple magic tricks or optical illusions to your class to give them some ideas. Visit your school library or public library to find some suitable reference books about magic. Children may try some of the ideas from *Arthur's April Fool*, such as doing shadow tricks, telling jokes, and reading people's minds.

- Find out about some famous magicians. In one illustration Arthur is carrying a book about Houdini. Encourage your students to do some research to find out who Houdini was. Ask them to name some current magicians, such as David Copperfield. Discuss the difference between "slight of hand" magic and "big illusions."

- Make a "Reading Is Magic" bulletin board to celebrate reading, while keeping the magic theme from *Arthur's April Fool*. Display a large black top hat cut from tag board in the center of the bulletin board. Make several small rabbits from white construction paper. Arrange them so they appear to be coming out of the hat. On each rabbit you could write the titles of the books you read to your class during the month.

- Look closely at the Joke Shop illustration in *Arthur's April Fool* with your students. Notice the unusual items. Students may then do some "Magic Shop Math" on page 103. You may have students use real coins and set up a Magic Shop in your classroom.

- Talk about several of Marc Brown's other Arthur books. Read them to your class and add some of them to your classroom library. Encourage your students to use their observation skills and become detectives searching for the names of Mr. Brown's sons in many of his books, as the back cover of *Arthur's April Fool* suggests.

- Make a class picture graph showing your students' favorite Arthur book. First, list several of their favorite Arthur books on your graph. Children may draw Arthur heads on 2" (5 cm) square pieces of white paper to use in marking favorite book choices on the graph.

Magic Shop Math

Use the price chart to find the total amount of money needed to buy the items in each hat. Write the answer in the hat.

Just a Dream

Author: Chris Van Allsburg

Publisher: Houghton Mifflin, 1990

Summary: This book sends a powerful message about the importance of the environment. In a dream, a boy travels to a future world full of pollution and environment problems.

Related Holiday: Earth Day was first held in the United States on April 22, 1970, and was founded by United States Senator Gaylord Neslon. The second Earth Day, held on April 22, 1990, was celebrated in over 140 countries. Earth Day is a day to remind us of the need to care for our environment. Another related holiday held nationally in the United States on the last Friday of April is Arbor Day, a day to plant new trees and emphasize conservation. It was first held in Nebraska on April 10, 1872, and its founder was conservation advocate Julius Sterling Morton. The date for Arbor Day may vary depending on the state in which you live.

Related Poetry: ''Hug a Tree Today'' by Susan M. Paprocki, *Special Day Celebrations* (Warren Publishing House, 1989), ''Nature Is'' by Jack Prelutsky, *The Random House Book of Poetry for Children* (Random House, 1983)

Related Song: ''It's Arbor Day Today'' by Elizabeth McKinnon and ''Trash Song'' by Carol Mellott, *Special Day Celebrations* (Warren Publishing House, 1989)

Connecting Activities:

- Assess students' knowledge of environmental issues by completing a word web using the word ''pollution'' or ''environment.'' Discuss the different types of pollution that exist in the world, especially any problems that are prevalent in your own community.

- Do a story map listing all the environmental events in the boy's dream. Have students write a sentence for each part of the story and illustrate it with crayon or marker. Tell where the boy went in each part of his dream. Ask the students if they noticed anything the same on each page. Remind them to look carefully, as the boy's cat follows him throughout the dream.

- Make a list of all the environmental mistakes that the boy saw during his dream. Discuss any unfamiliar vocabulary which relates to the book, such as wetlands and protected areas. Divide the class into small groups of four or five students. Assign each group one of the environmental mistakes. Have them discuss the mistake and come up with a list of possible solutions to the problem. Each group should make a detailed plan of action describing exactly what they would do.

Just a Dream (cont.)

- Discuss the informational book *50 Simple Things Kids Can Do To Save the Earth* by the Earthwork Group (see bibliography, page 118). See how many ideas your class can think of to save the earth. Compare your ideas to the ones found in the book. Put a star by any of the ideas which are already being implemented in your school or community.

- Each year the National Wildlife Federation produces a packet of classroom materials for use on Earth Day. The packet contains a teacher's guide, stamps, and an attractive poster showing the theme for Earth Day that year. Make a large banner that says "Earth Day EveryDay." Decorate the banner with crayons or markers, drawing some of the many ways we can help our planet each day.

- An excellent resource book is available for this holiday called *Earth Day* by Linda Lowery (see bibliography, page 118). This book describes the history of the foundation of Earth Day and gives many examples of ways in which people all over the world are working to improve our environment. The back of the book contains a list of environmental awareness ideas that children can follow at home, at play, and at school. A list of addresses for environmental organizations is also provided.

- Check to see if your school and community have recycling programs. Your school can recycle items such as certain types of paper and cafeteria lunch trays. Some communities have curbside recycling for items such as newspapers, cans, and plastic bottles. If such a program is not already in place, work with students to start recycling in your school. Contact local officials to urge them to start a community program. Teach the students how to make their own recycled paper by using the steps outlined in *50 Simple Things Kids Can Do To Save the Earth*.

- Students can write letters to city officials, senators, representatives, and even the president, urging them to pass laws which protect the environment. Have them include some of their concerns and ideas for possible solutions.

- Create a bulletin board entitled "Our Dreams for Our Environment." Divide the board into halves labeled "good dreams" and "bad dreams." On the good side, put paintings or drawings which represent a clean, safe environment. On the bad side, put illustrations to represent what will happen to the environment if we don't take better care of the earth.

- Make a book to show some of the ways we can make everyday an earth day. Color and cut out the cover provided on page 106 for your Earth Day book.

- The first Arbor Day was celebrated in Nebraska on April 10, 1872. Although recognized on different days throughout the country, you may wish to celebrate it with Earth Day activities. Have someone from a forestry service or conservation group visit your class to talk about the importance of replanting trees. If possible, arrange with your parent teacher organization to purchase seedlings for each student to take home and plant. Gather together the student population and plant a tree on school property.

Earth Day Book Cover

See page 105 for directions.

A Family in Japan

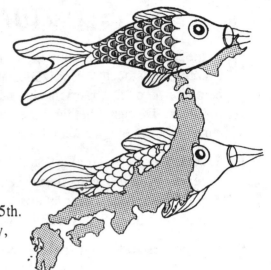

Author: Judith Elkin

Publisher: Lerner Publications Company, 1986

Summary: Explore the daily life of the Tomita family through the many color photographs which illustrate this book. The book also contains maps, a glossary, and a fact page about Japan.

Related Holiday: Children's Day is held in Japan on May 5th. This holiday used to be known as Boy's Day. Another holiday, called Doll's Day (March 3rd), was a special day for girls.

Related Poetry: ''Haiku'' by Gaki and ''Haiku'' by Yayu, *Tomie dePaola's Book of Poems* (G. P. Putnam's Sons, 1988)

Related Songs: ''Hina Matsuri Song'' by Elizabeth McKinnon, and ''Boy's Day Song'' by Jean Warren, *Small World Celebrations* (Warren Publishing House, 1989)

Connecting Activities:

- Prior to reading the story, bring in some informational texts about Japan. Locate Japan on a map or globe and ask students what they know about the country. If background knowledge is weak, you might want to show study prints, or a filmstrip, movie, or videotape on Japan.

- After reading the story, make a chart comparing a family in Japan to a family in America. Be sure to compare the following items: capital, language, form of money, area, population, alphabet, favorite food, religion, and popular sports.

- Create a special corner about Japan in your classroom. You might want to put the items on a low table and have the children sit on pillows as they do in Japan. Explain the custom of taking off shoes as a sign of respect and ask them to remove their shoes before they enter the area. Japanese homes often have a nature corner with flowers and paintings, called a tokonoma (toh-koh-NO-ma), so include that in the center also. Some other items to put in this area might include Japanese dolls, fans, origami, and any other items you can collect.

- As a homework assignment, ask students to locate items in their homes that are made in Japan. They may bring in the items to share or bring a list or a picture if the items are too large. See if students can name Japanese companies that manufacture items popular in the United States (Hitachi, Toyota, Suzuki, and Honda).

- When the Japanese children eat lunch at school, some of the typical foods are milk, fried noodles, bread, cheese, a tomato, and sometimes rice curry. Compare that lunch to a typical cafeteria lunch in America. Look at your school lunch menu and talk about how each lunch should have items from the four basic food groups. List five or six of the most popular entrees at the bottom of a piece of chart paper or on a bulletin board and do a picture graph to find out which lunch is the class favorite.

A Family in Japan *(cont.)*

- In the Japanese lunch room, there are many special rules that the children have to follow. For example, all students wear white hats and aprons, they brush their teeth after lunch, and they help to sweep the classroom and hallways. Compare and contrast your lunch rules with those in the story. Discuss whether there are rules that the students feel are needed which are not currently used in your school.

- Several forms of martial arts are very popular in Japan including a method of sword fighting called Kendo. In Japan, discipline and training are stressed as opposed to fighting. Have a guest speaker from a martial arts school come in and talk to the class about the rigorous training of mind and body that is really a part of these activities.

- The Japanese art of writing characters with brush strokes is referred to as calligraphy in the book. Try some calligraphy with your class. Start out by bringing in examples of this form of lettering which is very popular and can be found on everything from magazines and product labels to greeting cards. Have a calligrapher visit your class to show and demonstrate a few of the styles of lettering.

- Another Japanese art form which has become popular in other countries is origami, the art of paper folding. You can find many books at your local library which show simple projects that even a beginner can accomplish. Have students make origami items and hang them around the classroom.

- Fish kites are hung outside Japanese homes and are a symbol of strength, energy, and a long life. To make a simple version of this kite, reproduce the fish pattern on page 110 onto white paper. Enlarge the pattern for larger kites. Take tissue paper squares brushed with watered down glue and cover the fish by overlapping the squares. Attach paper streamers to the tail and a string at the top to complete the kite.

- Doll's Day is also part of the celebration. The doll pattern on page 109 can be decorated by students to create a unique doll. Students may bring in their own dolls to share with the class.

- Both the fish and doll shapes mentioned above could be used as a cover for a class book called "If I Lived in Japan." For more activities on Japan including a mini-fact book see TCM345 *Connecting Social Studies & Literature.*

Doll Pattern

Enlarge and use with the activities on page 108.

Fish Pattern

Enlarge and use with the activities on page 108.

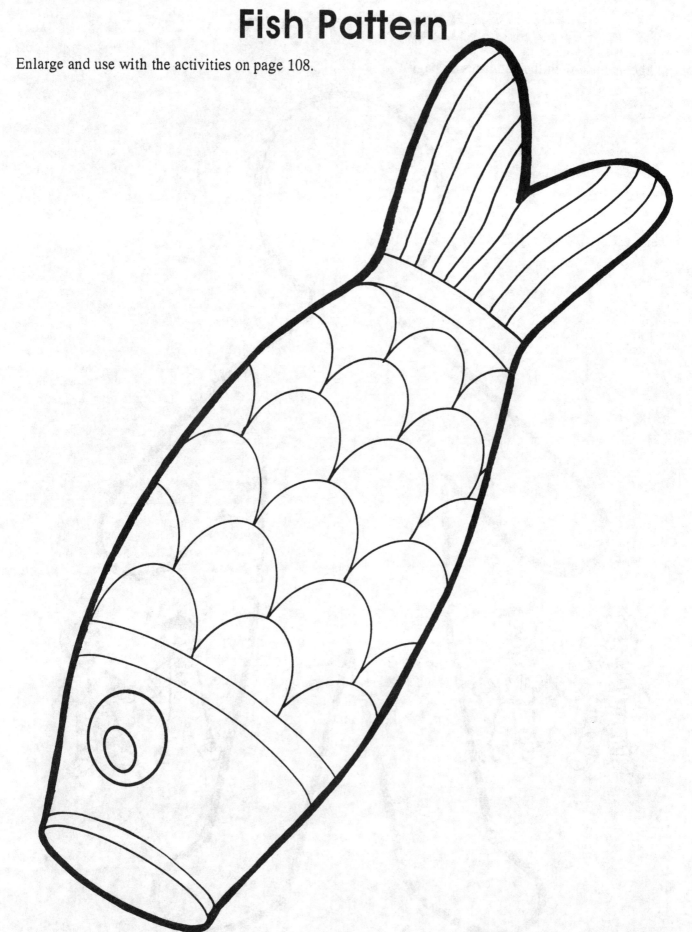

Fiesta!

Author: June Behrens

Publisher: Childrens Press, 1978

Summary: This colorful photo essay shows children enjoying a variety of Cinco de Mayo activities. The book details the history of the holiday and describes everything from a piñata party to a taco eating contest.

Related Holiday: Cinco de Mayo, the fifth of May is celebrated in Mexico and in the United States by Mexican Americans. It commemorates a battle won by Mexico against the French on May 5, 1862, which culminated in Mexico's independence.

Related Songs: ''Here Is Our Piñata'' by Elizabeth McKinnon, *Small World Celebrations* (Warren Publishing House, 1988); ''It's Cinco de Mayo Today'' by Elizabeth McKinnon, *Special Day Celebrations* (Warren Publishing House, 1989)

Connecting Activities:

- Locate Mexico on a world map or globe and discuss its location in North America. Talk about what Cinco de Mayo means and mention that it is celebrated on the same day as Children's Day in Japan. Cinco de Mayo can also be compared to May Day which is celebrated in many countries around the world. Cinco de Mayo commemorates an important milestone in Mexico's battle for independence.

- During the month of May, celebrate Hispanic culture with a variety of activities. List all of the countries in which Spanish is the primary language. Locate these on a map or globe. Do some research on Mexico's history including the explorers who came there from other lands.

- Learn some basic Spanish during the month of May. Some ideas to try are learning numbers, colors, days of the week, months of the year, hello and goodbye, thank you, and other simple conversational phrases. Invite a Spanish teacher or Spanish speaking parent to conduct some mini-language lessons. Each day, learn five Spanish words for items in the classroom. Attach hand printed word cards to the objects and repeat the words daily. Occasionally, remove and mix up some of the cards. Have students put them back in the correct sports. At the end of the month, have students draw a map of the classroom and label as many of the objects as they can in Spanish. Check your local teacher's store for charts printed in Spanish and other bilingual materials.

- Play some Mexican music in the background while reading *Fiesta!* Bring in some of the items mentioned in the story such as a sombrero, piñata, and maracas.

- Make a list of the Spanish words found in the book. Reproduce and cut out several copies of the sombrero on page 113 to make a picture dictionary. Print a different Spanish word on each page and then draw a picture to go with it. Staple the sombreros together for a Spanish picture dictionary.

Fiesta! (cont.)

- The book contains many photographs of Cinco de Mayo activities in an elementary school. One classroom picture shows a bulletin board about Mexico featuring a large map. Try duplicating the activity in your school by first making a large outline of the shape of Mexico. Students can then work in small groups to print the names of cities on cards. The cards are pinned in the correct location on the map. If you have access to any small souvenirs (pictures, postcards, craft items), pin these on the map also. Students could draw pictures with crayon or marker which show some additional features of Mexico.

- Look at some pictures of the Mexican flag, which is green, white, and red. Using tempera paint on white construction paper, the students can make their own flags. Staple or glue a craft stick to the edge to complete the flag. Compare the Mexican flag to flags of other countries which you have studied. Find out which countries use the same colors in their flags.

- Try some cooking with south of the border flair. Invite a parent to come in and cook some simple dishes with the class such as tortillas or tacos. Or, take a tour of a Mexican restaurant in your area. Tortilla chips are a simple but delicious favorite of most children. Try the tortilla chips different ways: plain, with melted cheese, with meat, and with meat and cheese. Other toppings may include lettuce, tomatoes, and sour cream. Do a picture graph or bar graph to find out which type of nacho is the most popular.

- Colorful piñatas are a part of many celebrations including Cinco de Mayo. Bring in different types of piñatas to show the class and talk about the many designs (stars, donkeys, sombreros). Create some new ideas for piñata designs and draw them with markers or use brightly colored paints.

- The sombrero pattern on page 113 can be enlarged for use on a bulletin board or as part of a cover for a class book. The book could show different aspects of this holiday celebrations. Or, enlarge the sombrero pattern on tag board and laminate. Using a wipe off pen, write a Spanish ''word of the day'' that you want to discuss with the class. Learn a new word each day during May.

- Organize a Cinco de Mayo fiesta in your classroom or school. Start by putting up colorful decorations such as red, white, and green streamers, banners, and the flags which the students painted. Try some of the activities shown in the book. Have a taco or nacho eating contest. Set up some fiesta booths decorated with streamers and tissue flowers. One photograph shows a bean bag toss game and an archaeological dig. Plan some other simple games with the students for your fiesta game booths, such as tossing a hoop over a sombrero. Be sure to play some mariachi music in the background during the fiesta. As the book says at its ending...''Viva la fiesta!''

Sombrero Pattern

See pages 111 and 112 for directions.

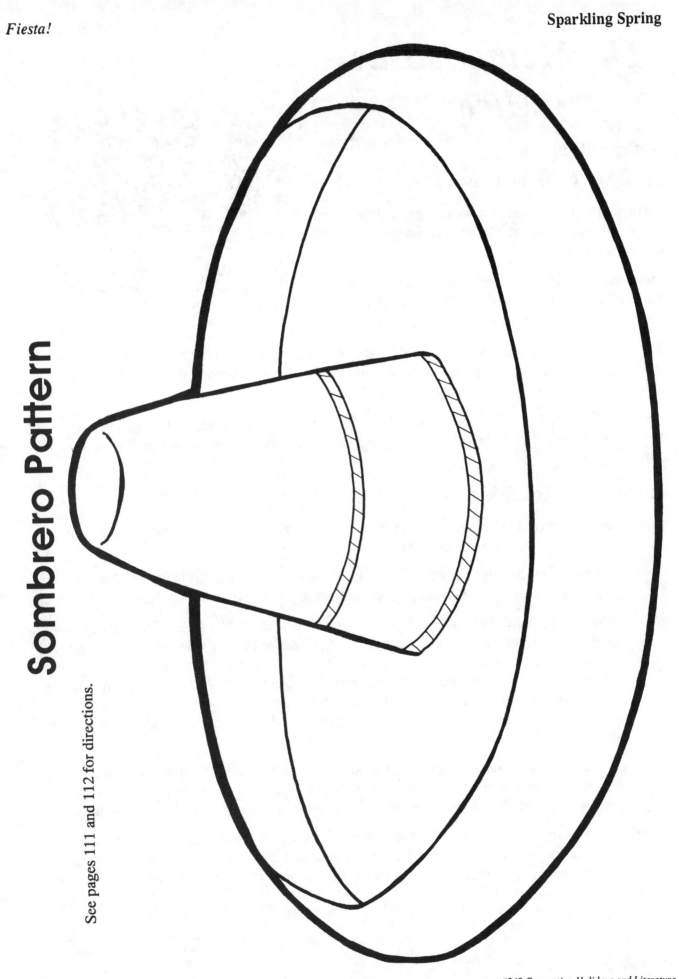

The Mother's Day Mice

Author: Eve Bunting

Publisher: Clarion Books, 1986

Summary: In this fantasy adventure, three little mice leave their house to search for the perfect gift for Mother on Mother's Day.

Related Holiday: Mother's Day is celebrated as a holiday in the United States and Canada to honor mothers and is held on the second Sunday in May.

Related Poetry: *Poems for Mothers* selected by Myra Cohn Livingston (Holiday House, 1988); ''Only One Mother'' by George Cooper and ''Mommies'' by Nikki Giovanni, *Poems and Rhymes* (World Book-Childcraft International, 1982)

Related Songs: ''It's Your Special Day'' by Sue Brown, ''Happy Mother's Day to You'' by Saundra Winnett and ''Mother's Day Song'' by Barbara Fletcher, *Holiday Piggyback Songs* (Warren Publishing House, 1988)

Connecting Activities:

- Before you read this book to your class, be sensitive to the feelings of your students whose mothers may no longer be in the home.

- As you are reading this book to your class, stop at the point when Little Mouse agrees to forget about the honeysuckle. Encourage your students to predict what ideas he has.

- After you have finished reading the book, work with your class to make a story grammar for the book. Since Little Mouse's gift was a song, write each of the story elements on large musical notes. Cut one musical note from a 12" x 18" (30 cm x 46 cm) construction paper for each of the following story elements: setting, characters, problems, events, resolution (solution), and theme. Display your story grammar musical notes on a bulletin board. Be sure to include the title of the book in your display, too. Children may each make torn-paper mice to add to the display.

- Discuss with your students whether this story is real or fantasy. Ask students to recall the clues that helped them decide that the story is fictional (clothing on mice, sleep in beds, wearing wristwatches, etc.). List these on a chart and look back in the book to check for accuracy.

- Make a three-column graph with the item each of the three mice (biggest, middle, littlest) gave to Mother shown at the bottom of the graph. Students show which of the three items they like best by placing a small heart cut from red construction paper in the corresponding column.

The Mother's Day Mice (cont.)

- Millions of Mother's Day cards are sent each year. Encourage your students to use markers, crayons, glitter, and sequins to create their own Mother's Day cards to take home or to present to their mothers at a "Mother's Day Tea" (see below).

- Have your students decide what they would like to give their mothers for Mother's Day. Have each child complete a page for a class book showing their perfect gift. Each child could complete a sentence starter, such as "The perfect gift for my mother would be..." to include on the page. Use page 117 as the cover for your book.

- Sing "Twinkle, Twinkle Little Star" with your class to remind them of the tune which Little Mouse used in writing his own song (found in the book). Encourage your students to write their own songs for Mother's Day following the same tune or pick out another classic tune to use. Children may sing their original songs, or ones listed at the beginning of these activities at a "Mother's Day Tea" (see below).

- Invite your students' mothers in for a special "Mom's Day" or a short "Mother's Day Tea." When your guests arrive in the classroom, students should start by introducing their guests. If a child's mother cannot attend, invite a grandmother, aunt, sister, or family friend to come in as that child's special guest. (You may need to use school personnel to fill vacancies.) During your tea, have the children sing their songs, recite related poetry or their own original poetry, and do a variety of activities to include the special guests: read a book together, make a picture together, do some manipulative math together, and then have a snack. The book *Super Snacks: Seasonal Sugarless Snacks for Young Children* by Jean Warren (see bibliography, page 144) would be a good source for healthy snack ideas. Children might also enjoy copying a recipe on a recipe card (see page 141) to use at home.

The Mother's Day Mice (cont.)

• Try some of these activities about real mice:

— Bring in a real mouse. Have students observe the mouse for five minutes, jotting down everything they see and hear in a Science Journal (see page 143). At the end of the observation, each child may choose one thing that they noticed to write about and illustrate for a class book. You might make your book in the shape of a mouse and attach a piece of yarn to it for a tail.

— Discuss the dangers which real mice face. How are real mice different from the mice in *The Mother's Day Mice*?

• Make a mouse bookmark from a 2" x 6" (5 cm x 15 cm) piece of construction or index paper and a 4" (10 cm) piece of yarn. Children cut out the mouse's body from the paper and add details with crayons or markers. Attach the yarn for a tail.

• Since mice like cheese, have a "Cheese Tasting Party." Include cheese from around the world and locate the countries of origin on a globe. Make a class graph of your favorite cheese.

• Make simple headbands from strips of 2" x 24" (5 cm x 61 cm) pieces of yellow construction paper. Staple the strips to fit each child's head. Cut out a piece of yellow paper and add black circles on it to resemble Swiss cheese. Children may write a sentence on the headband ("I read *The Mother's Day Mice* by Eve Bunting.") or facts about real mice.

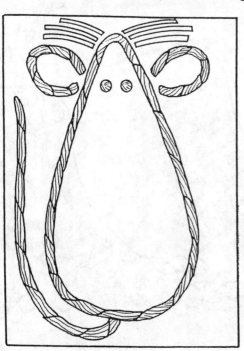

• Make mouse prints. Cut cardboard into 5" x 8" (12 cm x 20 cm) rectangular pieces (one per student). Draw an oval shaped mouse on the cardboard with a pencil. Place the string on top of the outline of the mouse and glue it down. Let it dry. Paint the string with thick tempera paint and quickly lay construction or typing paper on top of the string. Press down hard to make a print. If you have a rolling pin or round block, roll this over the paper. Remove paper and the mouse print will appear on your paper. This method can be used to make a variety of prints. Prints can then be used as decorations on cards, notes, flyers, etc.

Mother's Day Class Book Cover

Directions: Color this page and mount it on a piece of colorful tag board (making a border around the sheet). Use it as the cover for the class book titled "Our Perfect Mother's Day Gifts."

Sparkling Spring Bibliography

Adler, David A. *A Picture Book of Passover* (Holiday House, 1982)

Aldis, Dorothy. *Nothing Is Impossible — The Story of Beatrix Potter* (Atheneum, 1969)

Back, Christine & Jens Olesen. *Chicken and Egg* (Simon & Schuster, 1992)

Balian, Lorna. *Humbug Rabbit* (Humbug Press, 1974)

Balian, Lorna. *Leprechauns Never Lie* (Humbug Press, 1980)

Barth, Edna. *Lilies, Rabbits, and Painted Eggs: The Story of the Easter Symbols* (Clarion Books, 1970)

Barth, Edna. *Shamrocks, Harps, and Shillelaghs: The Story of the St. Patrick's Day Symbols* (Clarion Books, 1977)

Burns, Diane L. *Arbor Day* (Carolrhoda Books, 1989)

Carlson, Nancy. *Bunnies and Their Hobbies* (Puffin Books, 1984)

Cherry, Lynn. *The Great Kapok Tree* (HBJ, 1990)

Children's Television Workshop. *The Best of Sesame Street* (Children's Television Workshop, 1987)

Christian, Mary Blount. *April Fool* (Macmillan, 1981)

Collins, David R. *The Country Artist: A Story About Beatrix Potter* (Carolrhoda Books, 1989)

Crews, Donald. *Parade* (Morrow, 1987)

dePaola, Tomie. *Patrick: Patron Saint of Ireland* (Holiday House, 1992)

Dellinger, Annetta E. *My First Easter Book* (Childrens Press, 1985)

Earthworks Group, The. *50 Simple Things Kids Can Do To Save the Earth* (Andrews and McMeel, 1990)

Ehlert, Lois. *Eating the Alphabet: Fruits and Vegetables from A to Z* (HBJ, 1989)

Fisher, Aileen. *Arbor Day* (Thomas Y. Crowell, 1965)

Garza, Carmen Lomas. *Family Pictures* (Cuadros de Familia (Childrens Books Press, 1990)

Gibbons, Gail. *Easter* (Holiday House, 1989)

Gibbons, Gail. *The Post Office Book: Mail and How It Moves* (Trumpet, 1982)

Giff, Patricia Reilly. *Wake Up, Emily, It's Mother's Day* (Dell, 1991)

Heller, Ruth. *Chickens Aren't the Only Ones* (Scholastic, 1981)

Jacobsen, Karen. *Japan* (Childrens Press, 1982)

Jacobsen, Karen. *The Soviet Union* (Childrens Press, 1990)

Jacobsen, P. and Kirstensen, P. *A Family in Japan* (Watts, 1984)

Kroll, Steven. *Happy Mother's Day* (Holiday House, 1985)

LesTina, Dorothy. *April Fool's Day* (Follett, 1969)

LesTina, Dorothy. *May Day* (Thomas Y. Crowell, 1967)

Levine, Susan A. *Save Our Planet: 52 Easy Things Kids Can Do Now* (Parachute Press, 1990)

Lowery, Linda. *Earth Day* (Carolrhoda Books, 1991)

McRae, Patrick T. *Here Comes Peter Cottontail* (Ideals Publishing Company, 1985)

Merriam, Eve. *Mommies at Work* (Simon & Schuster, 1989)

Miller, Edna. *Mousekin's Easter Basket* (Simon & Schuster, 1986)

Plotkin, Gregory & Rita. *Cooking the Russian Way* (Lerner Publications, 1986)

Ryder, Joanne. *Under Your Feet* (Four Winds, 1990)

Scott, Geoffrey. *Memorial Day* (Carolrhoda Books, 1983)

Selsam, Millicent E. *Egg to Chick* (Harper & Row, 1970)

Shute, Linda. *Clever Tom and the Leprechaun* (Lothrop, Lee & Shepard, 1988)

Suyenaga, Ruth. *Korean Children's Day* (Modern Curriculum Press, 1992)

Wilhelm, Hans. *Bunny Trouble* (Scholastic, 1985)

Zalben, Jane Breskin. *Happy Passover, Rosie* (Holt, 1990)

A Perfect Father's Day

Author: Eve Bunting

Publisher: Clarion Books, 1991

Summary: This book tells the story of a little girl's unique, perfect day that she plans for herself and her father to celebrate Father's Day.

Related Holiday: Father's Day is celebrated on the third Sunday in June as the day to recognize how special fathers are.

Related Poetry: "Mummy Slept Late and Daddy Fixed Breakfast" by John Ciardi and "Daddy Fell into the Pond" by Alfred Noyes, *The Random House Book of Poetry for Children* (Random House, 1983)

Related Songs: "Father's Day" by Kristine Wagoner, "D-A-D" by Debra Lindahl, and "Gifts for Dad" by Patricia Coyne, *Holiday Piggyback Songs* (Warren Publishing House, 1988)

Connecting Activities:

- Before beginning these activities, be aware that some children in your class may not have fathers in their lives, in which case they could focus on a grandfather, uncle, or family friend.

- After reading this book to your students, discuss the way in which Susie handled the perfect day, while allowing her dad to do a few things. Make a comparison chart to show the things that Susie did (go out to eat, ride on toys at the park, get a balloon, etc.) and the things that Susie let her dad do (put her on park toys, buy balloon, drive, pay, etc.). Ask the children to decide who they would rather be, Susie or Dad.

- In the book, Susie planned the entire day for Dad. Make a list of Dad's favorite things to do and favorite places to go (fast food restaurant, duck pond, park, etc.) Have your students make a judgment as to whose favorite places they really were.

- Have your students evaluate the author's purpose in writing this book. Discuss why the author might have written this story and what its central theme is. Children might suggest ideas, such as to tell about ways to show fathers that they are loved. Have students identify what really made the day perfect for both Susie and Dad.

- Students may work in cooperative groups to create a story roll-up. Use a long piece of bulletin board paper. Each group of children could illustrate, in the correct sequence, one scene from the book (going out for lunch, the duck pond, the park, buying balloons, celebrating at home, etc.). When each group is finished, the long paper could be rolled up. To retell the story, slowly unroll the story as the children in each group narrate the events in each picture. Save your story roll-up to share with fathers at a Father's Day program (see page 120).

A Perfect Father's Day *(cont.)*

- Since Susie and Dad visited her favorite restaurant, make a graph of your students' favorite restaurants. Use students' prior knowledge to make your graph. Cut out the logo of each restaurant from advertisement material. Divide a large piece of tag board into several equal columns, saving room at the top for the graph title "Our Favorite Restaurant." Place each restaurant at the bottom of the columns on your graph. (You should leave one column free of logos and label it "Other" to accommodate children whose choices may not be used again. Children may each attach a sticky dot in the appropriate section to record their favorite restaurants. (These dots will come off the laminated surface if they are removed within a few days of doing the activity.)

- Students may plan their own special day to share with a father, grandfather, uncle, or friend, similar to Susie's day. Each child should include his or her favorite places to visit and things to do. Children could list their activities (with words and/or pictures) on a 12" x 24" (30 cm x 61 cm) piece of paper. Next to each activity place a blank clock face. On each clock face, have children add hands to show an approximate time when the activity should begin. A discussion of the length of time required for an activity will help your children record reasonable times. Title this sheet "A Perfect Day with _____" or "Our Perfect Father's Day." Roll up this sheet and tie it with a colorful ribbon as a special surprise for Dad.

- Students may paint portraits of their fathers to display on a bulletin board with a title, such as "Famous Dads from Room 3." Add a label to identify each father, such as "Jenna's Dad."

- Students may make greeting cards for their fathers on Father's Day. On the front cover of the card, children may draw a cake and add the number of candles needed to show how many years their father has been their father. Students may decorate their cards with items they think their dads would like for Father's Day. Add suitable text.

- Students may make a class book called "Our Perfect Fathers" in the shape of a big necktie (see page 121). Have each student do one page for the book in the same necktie shape, completing the sentence, "My father is perfect because _____." Attach the student pages to the cover and display the book during the culminating activity (see below).

- As a culminating activity, invite the fathers (or special guests) of your students into the classroom for a "Dad's Day" or short Father's Day program similar to that described for Mom's Day on page 115. Retell the story *A Perfect Father's Day* using the roll-up story, look at the perfect days the children planned for their fathers, read a book together, make a picture together, do some manipulative math together, and finish the day with a "Perfect Dad's Party."

Father's Day Class Book Cover

Directions: Color this page and mount it on a colorful piece of tag board (making a border around the sheet). Use it as the cover for your class book of ''Our Perfect Fathers.''

Fourth of July Bear

Author: Kathryn Lasky

Publisher: Morrow Junior Books, 1991

Summary: Enjoy the holiday festivities through the eyes of a young girl who gets to wear a special bear costume in a Fourth of July parade.

Related Holiday: The Fourth of July is the celebration of our country's independence in the year 1776. A similar holiday in Canada is Dominion Day, held on July 1st.

Related Poetry: "Fireworks" by Dorothy Aldis, *A Family Read-Aloud Holiday Treasury* (Little, Brown & Company, 1991); "Fourth of July" by Myra Cohn Livingston, *Celebrations* (Scholastic, 1985)

Related Songs: "America," "The Star Spangled Banner," "You're a Grand Old Flag," and "The Stars and Stripes Forever," *Wee Sing America* (Price/Stern/Sloan, 1987).

Connecting Activities:

- Prior to reading the story, have students predict what the story will be about, based on the title. As you read the story, talk about the different activities which characterize a Fourth of July celebration (parade, firework, etc.). Discuss which activities students have participated in on previous holidays.

- Organize a bicycle parade at your school. Have the children decorate their bikes with streamers, balloons, pictures, flags — anything red, white, and blue. Use the activity on page 125 to have students color and design their own bicycles for a parade. Encourage them to add lots of detail to the bicycles. If a bike parade is not possible in your area, have a patriotic pedestrian parade. The children can wear red, white, and blue hats, carry flags, and perhaps even play some small drums and cymbals.

- Put up three 12" x 18" (30 cm x 46 cm) pieces of construction paper; one red, one white, and one blue. Brainstorm a list of foods that are red, white, or blue. Use some of the foods named to make a menu for a Patriotic Picnic in your classroom. Spread out some colorful picnic cloths on the floor and enjoy your red, white, and blue buffet. You can prepare the food with the students or ask for help from parents. A sample menu might include: raspberry jam sandwiches, red fruit punch, blueberries, and vanilla ice cream.

- Study the United States flag, both in its current form and the different ways it has looked in the past (see bibliography, page 136). Have the students work in small cooperative groups to depict the different representations of the United States flag. The flags can be drawn and colored with crayons or markers. Put dates on the flags to show the year that they were used, and arrange the flags in chronological order. Use the activity on page 124 to create a "Mini-Book of U.S. Flags." Compare the United States flag to flags of other countries. Have students do research to see if any other countries have red, white, and blue in their flags.

Fourth of July Bear (cont.)

- Parades are a very popular part of any fourth of July festivities. Show students the wordless book by Donald Crews entitled *Parade* (see bibliography, page 136). Discuss with the children who and what might be in a parade. Have the class work together to create a mural of a parade. First, prepare a strip of blue butcher paper as a background. Add details such as brown paper for the ground and roads, green grass, trees, or whatever else the students want to add. Make construction paper characters to place in the scene. Some possibilities might be clowns with balloons, horses, floats, a band, and fire engines. Display the colorful mural in your classroom or hallway with a caption such as ''We're Marching Along in Room 2.'' Add some descriptive sentences to the mural. For example, ''Colorful clowns are carrying balloons.'' Or, change your mural into a number parade with 1 fire engine, 2 balloons, 3 clowns, etc.

- Clowns are a fun part of every parade, so arrange for a special clown theme day. Let the children put on some simple washable makeup to look like clowns and have them decorate construction paper cones for clown hats. If possible, arrange for a clown to visit the class and show how he or she puts on makeup. Talk about how clowns design their own makeup so that they have a unique look and show pictures of some famous clowns such as Emmett Kelly, Red Skelton, and Ronald McDonald.

- In this book, a beautiful fireworks display is part of the little girl's holiday. Try creating some fireworks on paper with this art project. Give each student a 9" x 12" (23 cm x 30 cm) piece of black construction paper. Using some brightly colored fluorescent paint, place small amounts of paint at random on the paper and blow with a straw to create your own ''fireworks.'' To add a collage effect to these pictures, cut out letters from magazines to spell descriptive words such as ''crash'' and ''boom.'' Place the words around your colorful fireworks display.

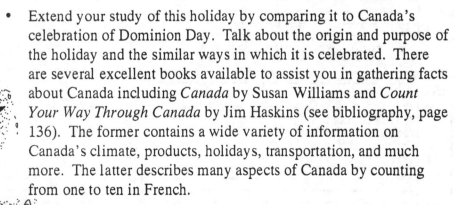

- Extend your study of this holiday by comparing it to Canada's celebration of Dominion Day. Talk about the origin and purpose of the holiday and the similar ways in which it is celebrated. There are several excellent books available to assist you in gathering facts about Canada including *Canada* by Susan Williams and *Count Your Way Through Canada* by Jim Haskins (see bibliography, page 136). The former contains a wide variety of information on Canada's climate, products, holidays, transportation, and much more. The latter describes many aspects of Canada by counting from one to ten in French.

Mini-Book of U.S. Flags

See page 122 for suggestions. Color the pictures in each box below. Cut out boxes, place the pages in order, and staple them.

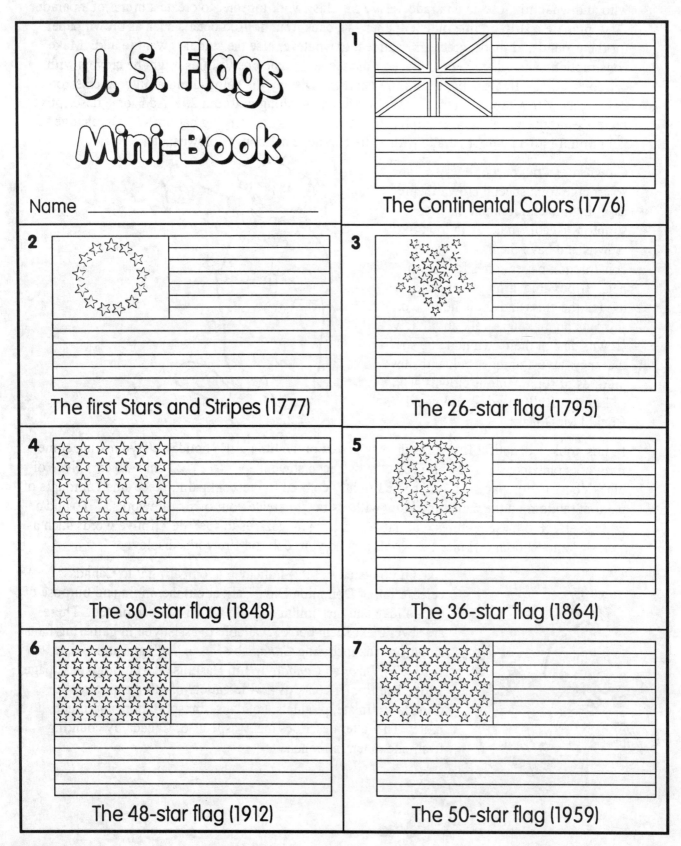

U. S. Flags Mini-Book

Name _____

1 The Continental Colors (1776)

2 The first Stars and Stripes (1777)

3 The 26-star flag (1795)

4 The 30-star flag (1848)

5 The 36-star flag (1864)

6 The 48-star flag (1912)

7 The 50-star flag (1959)

Bike Parade

Directions: Add details to this bike to make it one that you would like to ride in a bike parade.

Madeline

Author: Ludwig Bemelmans

Publisher: Scholastic, 1939

Summary: This Caldecott Honor book with rhyming text and beautiful paintings of Paris has become a classic for young children as they are introduced to Madeline and travel with her to the hospital where she has her appendix removed.

Related Holiday: Bastille Day was originally celebrated on July 14, 1789. Today, Bastille Day is celebrated in France to commemorate the taking of the Bastille (royal prison) which marked the beginning of the French Revolution with huge parades, fireworks, honoring of the flag, and singing the national anthem, making it similar to the Fourth of July in the United States.

Related Songs: ''La Marseillaise'' - the French national anthem: ''Frére Jacques'' - Traditional French version of ''Are You Sleeping?'' ''Hurray for Bastille Day'' by Vicki Claybrook, *Small World Celebrations* (Warren Publishing House, 1988)

Connecting Activities:

• Before reading this book to your students, explain to them that the setting of the book is Paris, France. Find Paris on a globe or world map.

• Read this book to your students to enjoy the story. Then do a story grammar on pieces of paper shaped like Madeline's hat. Make one hat shape each for the characters, the setting, the problem, the events, the resolution, and the theme.

• Use 6" x 12" (15 cm x 30 cm) pieces of paper on which your students may make get-well cards or write letters to Madeline to help cheer her up as she recovers from her appendicitis attack. Display them on a bulletin board with the title ''Madeline.'' Add some French travel brochures and pictures of Paris to your bulletin board.

• Compare Madeline's hospital and ambulance with a hospital and ambulance in your area. (Remind your students that Madeline was in Paris, France, in the 1930's.) Which things are the same? Which are different?

• Reread the book with your students and allow them to join in on the rhyming text. This time point out the various famous Paris landmarks in the book as you read. The Opera (setting for Phantom of the Opera), Colum Vendome, Hotel Ritz, the Hotel des Invalides, Notre Dame, Jardius (gardens) de Luxembourg, the river Seine, the Eiffel Tower, the Tuileries gardens, and the Lourve are all included in the illustrations. Have some reference books about Paris in your classroom for your students' independent research (see bibliography, page 136).

Madeline (cont.)

- Play the "Scenic Paris" game. Reproduce and attach pages 128 and 129 together to make the game board. Make copies of the game cards on page 130. (You may want to color these pages, mount them on tag board, and laminate them to increase their durability.) Players take turns drawing a card (each with the name of a Paris landmark) and moving to the next corresponding space which has a picture of that landmark. If possible, use tiny French flags standing on a colored ball of clay as markers. The winner is the child who arrives at Madame Clavel's school first. As a challenge, have players pronounce the landmark name on the chosen card before moving the game piece. (Or, tell a fact about the landmark.) Make new game cards, using French words or numbers. Students say these before moving markers.

- Discuss the illustrations done by the author/illustrator, calling your students' attention to the yellow background and use of a black line for drawing. Then give each of your students a piece of yellow construction paper on which they may use a black marker to sketch their favorite scene from the book (or a landmark in your own neighborhood).

- Make a poster of some French numbers and words for your classroom. Help your students learn to count to twelve in French so that they can count the twelve little girls in the book in French. Use the following information as your guide:

0 *zero* (zay-Ro)	**4** *quatre* (KahtR)	**8** *huit* (Ueet)
1 *un* (ER(n))	**5** *cinq* (sEHk)	**9** *neuf* (nERf)
2 *deux* (dER)	**6** *six* (sees)	**10** *dix* (dees)
3 *trois* (tRwah)	**7** *sept* (set)	**11** *onze* (OHz)
		12 *douze* (dooz)

- List after-school snacks that your students enjoy. Then tell your students about typical French after-school snacks, such as pain (pan) au chocolate (bread with a piece of chocolate baked in the middle), goutar aux raisins (bread stuffed with raisins), or chausson aux pommes (bread stuffed with apples).

- Discuss Bastille Day (called the Fourteenth of July in France) with your students by comparing it to the Fourth of July in the United States. Share with your students the ways that Bastille Day is celebrated: singing the national anthem, "La Marseillaise" (play a recording of it for your class); displaying the French flag; fireworks; military parades; different types of bands playing in the evening; dancing in the streets with famous stars appearing; picnics; and wearing a cocarde (co card), which is a pleated blue, red, and white badge.

- Use page 131 to have your students make cocardes to wear. Sometimes ribbons are attached and hung from the cocarde.

- Plan a picnic to sample a taste of some French foods, such as a croissant, a baguette (long loaf of bread), and some French cheeses (camembert and brie).

- Show your students the flag of France. Students may paint their own French flags. Divide a piece of 12" x 18" (30 cm x 46 cm) white construction paper into thirds, lengthwise. Paint the left third blue and the right third red, while leaving the middle third white.

"Scenic Paris"

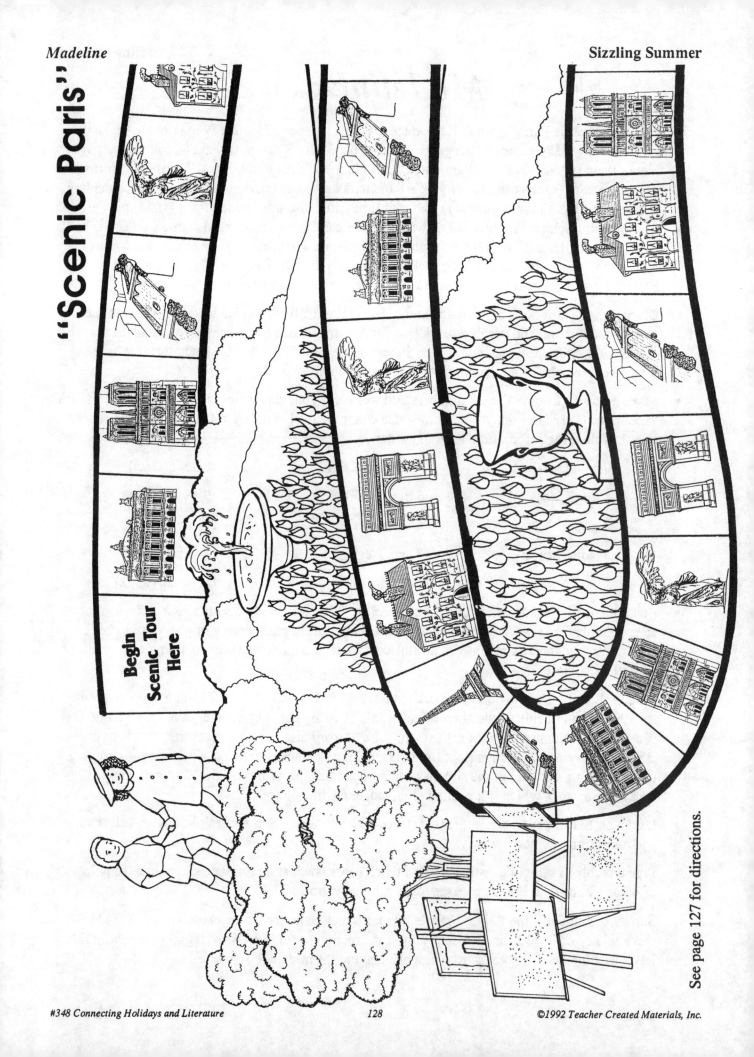

Begin Scenic Tour Here

See page 127 for directions.

Madame Clavel's School

Game Board

"Scenic Paris" Game Cards

Directions: Cut the cards along the dashed lines and use with the "Scenic Paris" Game Board.

Eiffel Tower	**Eiffel Tower**	**Eiffel Tower**	**Eiffel Tower**
Opéra	**Opéra**	**Opéra**	**Opéra**
Notre Dame	**Notre Dame**	**Notre Dame**	**Notre Dame**
Seine River	**Seine River**	**Seine River**	**Seine River**
Louvre	**Louvre**	**Louvre**	**Louvre**
Arc de Triomphe	**Arc de Triomphe**	**Arc de Triomphe**	**Arc de Triomphe**
Madame Clavel's School	**Madame Clavel's School**	**Madame Clavel's School**	**Madame Clavel's School**

A French Cocarde

Directions: Use blue, red, and white to make this cocarde to wear in celebration of the Fourteenth of July (Bastille Day).

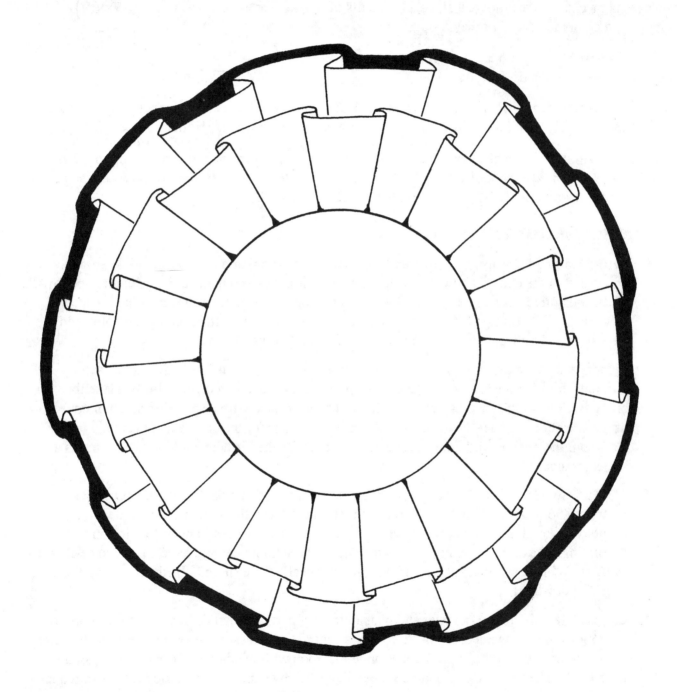

Happy Birthday!

Author: Gail Gibbons

Publisher: Holiday House, 1986

Summary: Learn the history of why and how birthdays are celebrated in this informative and colorful book. The book contains charts of astrological signs, plus charts of flowers and colors for each birthday month.

Related Holiday: A birthday is a special, personal holiday to celebrate the date of your birth.

Related Poetry: *Happy Birthday!*, an entire book of poems selected by Lee Bennett Hopkins (Simon and Schuster, 1991); "Birthday" by Myra Cohn Livingston, *Celebrations* (Holiday House, 1985)

Related Songs: "The Unbirthday Song" by Mack David, Al Hoffman, and Jerry Livington, *The New Disney Illustrated Songbook* (Harry N. Abram, Incorporated, 1986); *Happy Birthday*, a tape of birthday songs by Sharon, Lois, and Bram (Elephant Records, 1988)

Connecting Activities:

- Before reading the story, give each child a party hat, balloon, or a horn as a story keepsake. Discuss with the children how they celebrate their birthdays and make a list on chart paper of all the birthday traditions that they can think of. For example, some families may have a special favorite meal at home, while others may go out to a restaurant. After reading the book, add to the list any additional ideas found in the story for celebrating birthdays.

- Celebrate the birthday of each child in your classroom as a personal holiday. Give each birthday child a birthday certificate, a balloon, or a crown decorated with glitter. Have the birthday child sit in a birthday chair, which can be decorated with a special cushion or cover, or tissue streamers. Or, let the child sit in the teacher's chair for the day. Have everyone in the class sign their names and draw pictures on a banner for the birthday child to take home as a remembrance.

- Take a field trip to your local bakery to see a demonstration of cake decorating. Or, have a pastry chef or cake decorator come to the classroom to teach the students how to decorate a birthday cake. Bake some cupcakes and have the students try their hand at frosting and decorating. Make the cupcakes toward the end of the school year and have a party to celebrate everyone's birthday, or use the occasion to celebrate all of the summer birthdays. Sing the "Unbirthday Song."

- Choose a favorite book character and plan a birthday party for that character. Make appropriate invitations, treats, and decorations to follow a central theme associated with the book character. For example, try a birthday party for Winnie the Pooh with the theme, "Have a honey of a birthday." The invitations might be shaped like a beehive and say "Christopher Robin requests the honor of your presence at a birthday party for his friend, Winnie the Pooh." The room could be decorated to look like the Hundred Acre Woods. Treats of biscuits and honey, or honey drop cookies could be served. Other character themes might include Clifford, Curious George, or Madeline.

Happy Birthday! (cont.)

- Try a variety of birthday topics for class graphs. Using the *Happy Birthday!* book, look up the flower or birthstone for each student. The information could then be displayed as a picture graph or bar graph. It is also fun to have the students find out their birth weight and length. The weights could be done on a bar graph, and the lengths could be represented by strings and arranged in order from shortest to longest. Compare the birth weight and height to their current weight and height. Subtract the numbers to see how much they've grown.

- Another idea for graphing involves the use of a real graph. First, lay a large cloth or sheet of vinyl on the floor. Provide a cupcake for each student. Record each student's birth date on a paper candle, affix it to a toothpick, and put one in each cupcake. Roll out the floor graph and graph birthdays by the season in which they appear. One final "delicious" graph would be to have the students choose their favorite cake batter, chocolate, white, or yellow. Make a real graph using the actual cupcakes, or fill in a picture or bar graph.

- Do some scientific observations of a birthday candle that has been lit by the teacher. Prior to lighting the candle, predict how long it will take the candle to burn out. While the candle is burning, have the students write down everything that they observe about the candle in a science journal. You might also have someone demonstrate the art of candle making with your students, or visit a facility such as a nature center or a homestead farm that might have a demonstration.

- How about some birthday math fun? Have each student interview five friends to find out their birth dates. The students then subtract the birth date from the current date to find out their friend's age in years and months. This type of math problem also develops calendar skills.

- Talk with students about the steps involved in making a birthday cake. Start by brainstorming a list of possible ingredients, and then talk about a probable sequence. Read a cake recipe from a cookbook to check your ideas. Use the mini-book on pages 134-135 to sequence the directions for *How to Bake a Birthday Cake*. Have students color the pictures on each mini-page. Cut the mini-pages along the dashed lines. Staple the book together after putting the pages in the correct order. The correct steps are: mix butter and sugar; add eggs and vanilla; put in flour, baking powder, and salt; stir the cake batter; put the batter in a pan and bake; add frosting and decorations; enjoy!

- For a beginning of the school year idea, have each student draw the name of another student. Those students become "Birthday Buddies" for the year. On their buddy's birthday, the students bring in a treat. This is a fun idea that works well with the adult staff in your school building, too!

Mini-Sequence Book

See page 133 for directions.

How To Bake a Birthday Cake

Add eggs and vanilla.

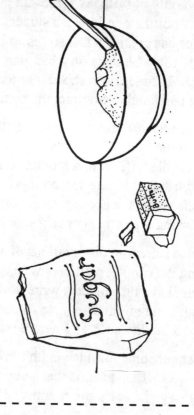

Mix butter and sugar.

Baker: _____

Author's Name

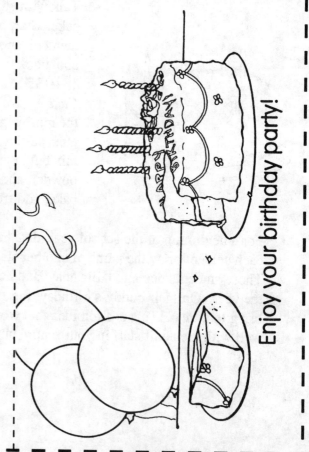

Enjoy your birthday party!

Mini-Sequence Book (cont.)

See page 133 for directions.

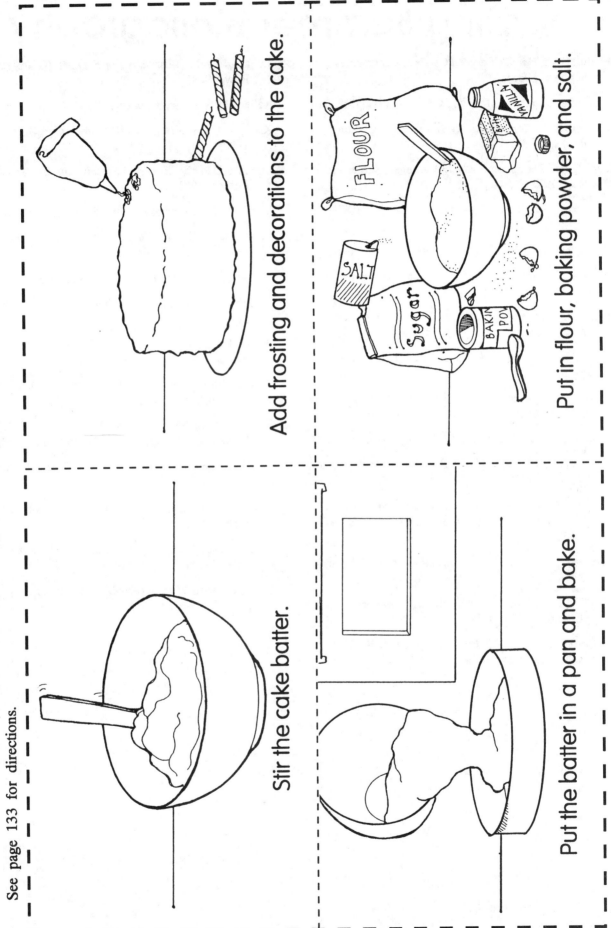

Add frosting and decorations to the cake.

Put in flour, baking powder, and salt.

Stir the cake batter.

Put the batter in a pan and bake.

Sizzling Summer Bibliography

Baylor, Byrd. *I'm in Charge of Celebrations* (Charles Scribner, 1986)

Bemelmans, Ludwig. *Madeline's Rescue* (Viking, 1953)

Bunting, Eve. *Happy Birthday, Dear Duck* (Clarion Books, 1988)

Carle, Eric. *The Secret Birthday Message* (Harper and Row, 1972)

Champion, Neil. *Countries of the World Facts* (EDC Publishing, 1986)

Crews, Donald. *Parade* (Morrow, 1986)

Fowler, Susi Gregg. *When Summer Ends* (Greenwillow Books, 1989)

Fradin, Dennis B. *The Flag of the United States* (Children's Press, 1988)

Hoban, Russell. *A Birthday for Frances* (Harper & Row, 1968)

Holabird, Katharine. *Angelina's Birthday Surprise* (Crown Publishing, 1989)

Galdeish, Alice. *The Fourth of July Story* (Aladdin, 1987)

Geisel, Theodor Seuss. *Happy Birthday To You!* (Random House, 1958)

Giblin, James Cross. *Fireworks, Picnics, and Flags: The Story of the Fourth of July Symbols* (Clarion Books, 1983)

Hallinan, P.K. *Today Is Your Birthday!* (Ideals Publishing, 1990)

Haskins, Jim. *Count Your Way Through Canada* (Carolrhoda Books, 1989)

Hodgson, Harriet W. *My First Fourth of July Book* (Childrens Press, 1987)

Hoban, Russell. *A Birthday For Frances* ((Harper and Row, 1968)

Keller, Holly. *Henry's Fourth of July* (Greenwillow, 1985)

Kiser, SuAnn & Kevin. *The Birthday Thing* (Greenwillow, 1990)

Liftshitz, Danielle. *France: The Land and Its People* (Silver Burdett, 1981)

Merriam, Eve. *Daddies at Work* (Simon & Schuster, 1989)

Moss, Peter & Thelma Palmer. *Enchantment of the World: France* (Childrens Press, 1986)

Munsch, Robert. *Moira's Birthday* (Annick Press, 1987)

Norbrook, Dominique. *Passport to France* (Franklin Watts, 1986)

Parker, Kristy. *My Dad the Magnificent* (Dutton Children's Books, 1987)

Passport Books. *Let's Learn French Picture Dictionary* (NTC Publishing Group, 1991)

Perl, Lila. *Candles, Cakes, and Donkey Tails: Birthday Symbols and Celebrations* (Clarion Books, 1984)

Schick, Eleanor. *One Summer Night* (Greenwillow Books, 1977)

Shactman, Tom. *America's Birthday: The Fourth of July* (Macmillan, 1986)

Spurr, Elizabeth. *The Biggest Birthday Cake in the World* (HBJ, 1991)

Stock, Catherine. *Birthday Present* (Bradbury Press, 1991)

Holiday Handbook Cover

Directions: Cut out and glue this cover on a 9" x 12" (23 cm x 30 cm) piece of construction paper or tag board. Use with pages 138-140.

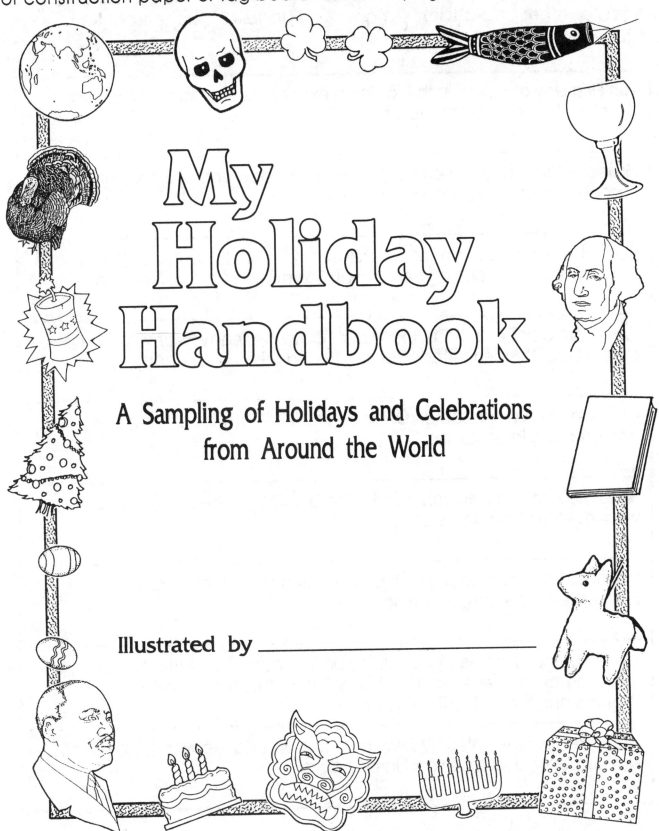

My
Holiday
Handbook

A Sampling of Holidays and Celebrations
from Around the World

Illustrated by _____

Holiday Handbook

Directions: Cut apart these strips. Put one strip at the bottom of a sheet of 9" x 12" (23 cm x 30 cm) paper. Illustrate this holiday. Put the holiday pages together and attach the cover on page 137 to the front for a Holiday Handbook.

The First Day of School in the fall is an exciting celebration for children, their families, and their teachers.

Grandparents' Day is a day to honor all grandparents. It is held on the second Sunday in September.

Columbus Day is celebrated on October 12th. On this date in 1492, Christopher Columbus landed on San Salvador in Central America.

Celebrate October 27th as Teddy Bear Day. The Teddy Bear was named after a U.S. President, Teddy Roosevelt, and this is his birthday.

Halloween is celebrated on October 31st. It is a day for carving pumpkins and dressing in costumes.

Sandwich Day on November 3rd is the birthday of the Earl of Sandwich, who invented the sandwich.

National Children's Book Week is celebrated during the third week in November to celebrate reading.

Thanksgiving is the national holiday on the fourth Thursday in November to remember the feast held in 1621 in Plymouth, Massachusetts, by the Pilgrims and the Native Americans.

Hanukkah is celebrated by Jewish people around the world. It comes in November or December and lasts 8 days.

Holiday Handbook *(cont.)*

See page 138 for directions.

Christmas is a Christian holiday celebrated on December 25th.

Kwanzaa is a holiday begun in 1966 to honor African-Americans and their history. It lasts from December 26th to January 1st.

New Year's Day is celebrated all around the world on different dates.

Martin Luther King, Jr. Day is celebrated in the United States on the third Monday in January to honor civil rights leader Dr. Martin Luther King, Jr.

The Chinese New Year comes between the middle of January and the middle of February. It is the Chinese celebration of the New Year and lasts seven days.

Groundhog Day is celebrated on February 2nd. The groundhog comes out of hibernation on this date and predicts when spring will arrive.

President's Day is celebrated on the third Monday in February to honor two U.S. Presidents, George Washington and Abraham Lincoln.

Valentine's Day is celebrated on February 14th as a day for honoring friends and the ones we love.

St. Patrick's Day is celebrated on March 17th to honor the Irish St. Patrick.

Holiday Handbook *(cont.)*

See page 138 for directions.

Easter is a Christian holiday celebrated in March or April.

April Fool's Day is April 1st. It is a day for practical jokes.

Earth Day is celebrated on April 22nd around the world to learn more about taking care of the earth.

Cinco de Mayo is a Mexican holiday celebrated on May 5th with a fiesta.

Children's Day is celebrated in Japan on May 5th as a special day for children.

Mother's Day is celebrated on the second Sunday in May to honor mothers.

Father's Day is celebrated on the third Sunday in June to honor fathers.

The Fourth of July is celebrated in the United States as the day it declared its independence from England.

Bastille Day is celebrated in France on July 14th.

Birthdays are each person's special holiday to celebrate.

My birthday is on _____.

Classy Cookery

by Chef _____

We read the book _____

We made _____

Ingredients:

_____   _____   _____

_____   _____   _____

Directions:

_____

_____

Poetry Pocket

Use the poem "Keep a Poem in Your Pocket" by Beatrice Schenk de Regniers (*The Random House Book of Poetry for Children*, selected by Jack Prelutsky, Random House, 1983) to introduce this activity.

Directions: Color and cut out the pocket on this page. Put glue around its edges and mount it on construction paper or tag board. Copy and store any appropriate poems you like in your "Poetry Pocket."

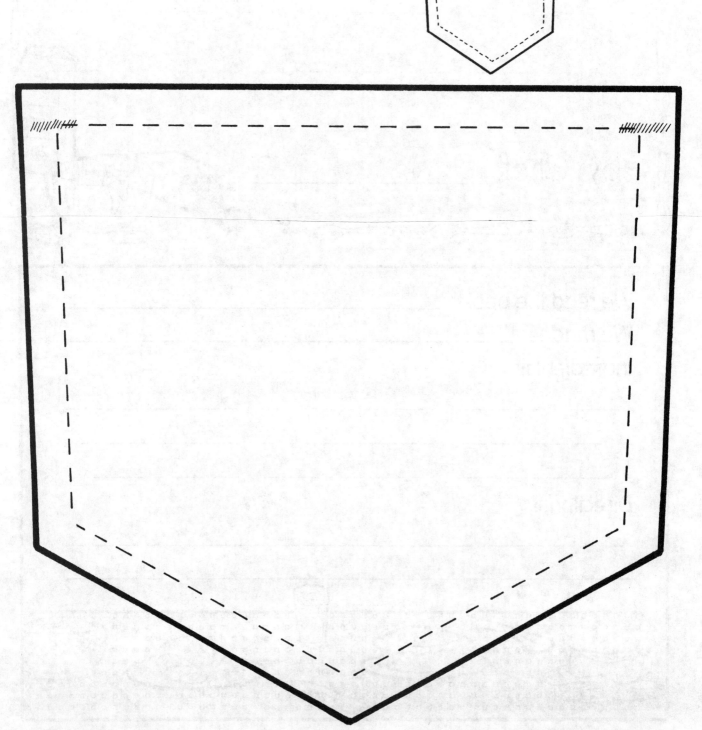

My Science Journal

Date: _____

Title of Activity: _____

What I want to find out: _____

_____

_____

What I think will happen: _____

_____

_____

What I observed: _____

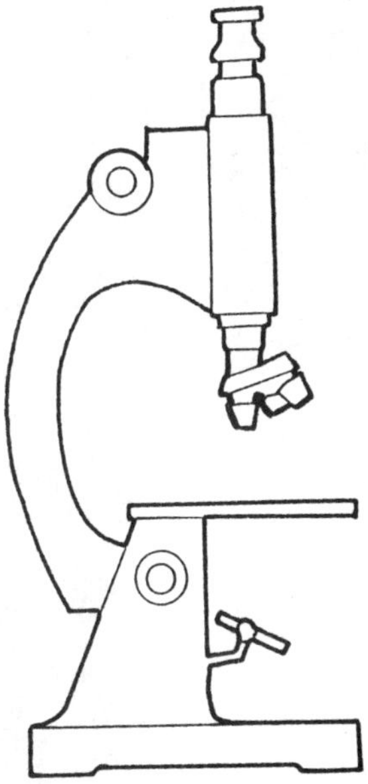

_____

_____

_____

_____

_____

Teacher Resources

Bibliography

Greene, Carol. *Holidays Around the World* (Childrens Press, 1982)

Harelson, Randy. *Amazing Days* (Workman, 1979)

Hautzig, Esther. *Holiday Treats* (Macmillan, 1983)

Higgins, Susan Olson. *The Elves' Christmas Book* (Pumpkin Press Publishing House, 1986)

Hopkins, Lee Bennett & Misha Arenstein. *Do You Know What Day Tomorrow Is? A Teacher's Almanac* (Scholastic, 1990)

Johnson, Barbara. *Cup Cooking: Individual Child-Portion Picture Recipes* (Early Educators Press, 1978)

Klutz, Press. *Kids Cooking: A Very Slightly Messy Manual* (Klutz Press, 1987)

Low, Alice. *The Family Read-Aloud Holiday Treasury* (Little, Brown & Company, 1991)

McKinnon, Elizabeth. *Special Day Celebrations* (Warren Publishing House, 1989)

Teacher Created Materials. *Connecting Science and Literature* (TCM341, 1991)

Teacher Created Materials. *Connecting Social Studies and Literature* (TCM345, 1992)

Teacher Created Materials. *Thematic Unit — Christmas* (TCM259, 1992)

Teacher Created Materials. *Thematic Unit — Halloween* (TCM257, 1992)

Teacher Created Materials. *Thematic Unit — Thanksgiving* (TCM258, 1992)

Teacher Created Materials. *Whole Language Units for Holidays* (TCM019, 1992)

Teacher Created Materials. *Big Book of Favorite Tales: Goldilocks and the Three Bears* (TCM550, 1992)

Van Straalen, Alice. *The Book of Holidays Around the World* (E.P. Dutton, 1986)

Warren, Jean. *Super Snacks: Seasonal Sugarless Snacks for Young Children* (Warren Publishing House, 1982)

Warren, Jean & McKinnon, Elizabeth. *Small World Celebrations* (Warren Publishing House, 1988)

Addresses

Dale Seymour Publications
P.O. Box 10888
Palo Alto, CA 94303-0879
Phone: (800) 872-1100

Modern Curriculum Press, Incorporated
13900 Prospect Road
Cleveland, OH 44136
Phone: (800) 321-3106

National Wildlife Federation
1400 16th Street Northwest
Washington D.C. 20036-2266

Oriental Trading Company
P.O. Box 3407
Omaha, NE 68103
Phone: (402) 331-5511

Treetop Publishing
2200 Northwestern Avenue
Racine, WI 53404-2519
Phone: (414) 633-9228

The Wright Group
19201 120th Avenue Northeast
Bothell, WA 98011-9512

Zoological Society of San Diego, Incorporated
P.O. Box 551
San Diego, CA 92112